/Feminine personality and conflict / Jud
HQ1206 .F43 1981 C.1 STACKS 1981

+HQ1206 .F43 1981

HQ	Feminine personality and
1206	conflict / Judith M.
F43	Bardwick
1981	

HQ	Feminine personality and
1206	conflict / Judith M.
F43	Bardwick
1981	

DATE	ISSUED TO
FEB 2 3 1992 JUL 1 4 1994	

DEMCO

feminine personality
and conflict

Contemporary Psychology Series
Edward L. Walker, Editor

The frontiers of psychology are advancing—advancing in response to persistent and fundamental social problems, advancing as a result of improved technology in both research and application, advancing through individual creative effort.

Brooks/Cole Publishing Company will make contemporary ideas, research, and applications widely available to students and scholars through the Contemporary Psychology Series.

Psychological Aspects of International Conflict
Ross Stagner, Wayne State University

An Anatomy for Conformity
Edward L. Walker, The University of Michigan,
and Roger W. Heyns, The University of California, Berkeley

Delinquent Behavior in an American City
Martin Gold, The University of Michigan

Feminine Personality and Conflict
Judith M. Bardwick, Elizabeth Douvan,
Matina S. Horner, and David Gutmann,
The University of Michigan

feminine personality
and conflict

Judith M. Bardwick

The University of Michigan

Elizabeth Douvan

The University of Michigan

Matina S. Horner

Radcliffe College

David Gutmann

The University of Michigan

GREENWOOD PRESS, PUBLISHERS
WESTPORT, CONNECTICUT

COLLEGE FOR HUMAN SERVICES
LIBRARY
345 HUDSON STREET
NEW YORK, N.Y. 10014

Library of Congress Cataloging in Publication Data

Main entry under title:

Feminine personality and conflict.

   Reprint of the ed. published by Brooks/Cole Pu
Co., Belmont, Calif., in series: Contemporary
psychology series.
   Includes bibliographies and index.
   1. Women--Psychology. 2. Femininity
(Psychology) I. Bardwick, Judith M., 1933-
[HQ1206.F43 1981]   155.6'33   80-2419
ISBN 0-313-22504-4 (lib. bdg.)

© 1970 by Wadsworth Publishing Company, Inc., Belmo,
California 94002.

All rights reserved. No part of this book may be reproducec
stored in a retrieval system, or transcribed, in any form or
by any means, electronic, mechanical, photocopying, recorc
ing, or otherwise, without the prior written permission of tl
publisher: Brooks/Cole Publishing Company, a division of
Wadsworth Publishing Company, Inc.

Photographs by Mike Powers.

Reprinted with the permission of Wadsworth Publishing
Company.

Reprinted in 1981 by Greenwood Press
A division of Congressional Information Service, Inc.
88 Post Road West, Westport, Connecticut 06881

Printed in the United States of America

10 9 8 7 6 5 4 3 2 1

series editor's preface

Civil rights for women is a recurrent and unresolved problem. The subject inspires activist disruption, scholarly effort, empirical research, party conversation, and political debate. Although the topic of equality of social opportunity for women tends to become figural in our society in every period of concern for civil rights for any group, the problem of women is quite different from that of any other oppressed group.

In most civil rights issues the tyranny of a majority effectively denies equal opportunity to a minority. However, females are in the majority, largely because of their longer lifespan. Thus civil rights for women is not a minority problem.

Most civil rights issues are tinged with economic problems. Blacks tend to be poor; thus their struggle is in part an effort to achieve equal economic opportunity and status. In contrast, women hold much more than half the wealth in the United States. The problems and conflicts associated with the feminist movement are not substantially economic in character.

Genetic arguments surround some civil rights issues. Although there seem to be some genetic differences between blacks and whites, the *relevance* of those differences to social and economic issues has not been established. With respect to civil rights for women, there is no question that there *are* genetic differences—those associated with sex and reproduction—that are *relevant* to the questions involved.

This book contains four chapters, each written by a psychologist and each addressed to some aspect of the biological and social problems associated with the status of women.

The first chapter, by Judith M. Bardwick, presents the results of research oriented to the development of a personality theory of women. The theory makes figural the common biological events that are uniquely feminine: menstruation, the development of breasts, childbirth, and lactation. Femininity is clearly associated with the female's attitudes toward her reproductive system and the sequence of changes it undergoes in normal development.

Elizabeth Douvan describes the characteristics and problems of the adolescent girl, especially those problems associated with the menarche. She emphasizes both physical and social factors that determine certain aspects of the feminine personality in this developmental period.

Matina S. Horner discusses research on the need for achievement in women. Her work is based on the empirical fact that the traditional measures of need for achievement (as developed by McClelland and Atkinson and their co-workers) function relatively well for men but relatively poorly for women. She has found that achievement orientation in women is blunted by a fear of success that appears to stem from a conflict between achievement and the feminine role.

David Gutmann's very insightful chapter orders some of the characteristics of the feminine ego on a dimension of strength with males and females in Indian cultures, with Hippies, and even with the effects of the drugs used in Indian and youth cultures.

The four chapters represent the independent, but partially integrated, contributions of four scholars, each of whose work adds positively to our understanding of the nature of feminine personality today and of the biological and social factors that contribute to the essence of femininity.

Edward L. Walker

contents

1
Psychological Conflict and the Reproductive System 3
Judith M. Bardwick

2
New Sources of Conflict in Females at Adolescence and Early Adulthood 31
Elizabeth Douvan

3
Femininity and Successful Achievement: A Basic Inconsistency 45
Matina S. Horner

4
Female Ego Styles and Generational Conflict 77
David Gutmann

Index 97

feminine personality
and conflict

1

psychological conflict and the reproductive system

Judith M. Bardwick

To a very large extent women *are* their bodies. In this essay I discuss three ideas: (1) the ambivalence that women in modern Western culture commonly feel toward the reproductive system, (2) psychosomatic changes in the reproductive system that act as psychological defenses, and (3) mood changes that are a direct result of the menstrual cycle. I conclude that women experience conflict about the sexual use of their body. They express that conflict in somatic symptoms in the reproductive system. They also experience conflict with different aspects of their personality in premenstrual feelings of anxiety, hostility, depression, and inadequacy.

Ambivalence toward the Reproductive System

It is fairly obvious that a woman's self-esteem and self-concept are more closely linked to the appearance and functioning of her body than is true for the man. Whereas masculinity is at least partially defined by success in marketplace achievements, femininity is largely defined by success in establishing and maintaining love relationships and by maternity. A woman's attractiveness is clearly instrumental in attracting men, and her self-evaluation as a woman will largely depend on her sexual and maternal success.

The menstrual cycle and pregnancy reinforce an awareness of internal reproductive functions. The obstetric and gynecological literature strongly supports the idea that women have a close psychological relationship to their reproductive system, which is a frequent site for the acting out of impulses, especially aggression and its derivatives, sex anxiety, and maternity-pregnancy fears. When we examine the dynamics of these psychosomatic behaviors, we find that they are closely linked to the level of the woman's self-esteem. There is, in women, a common psychological vulnerability that comes from low feelings of self-esteem, a strong and persistent need for respect from others in order to support self-esteem, and the fear of loss of love that could destroy self-esteem. A vulnerable sense of self-esteem—one that is dependent on appraisals from others—implies that there is no independent sense of self.

How can we understand this apparently curtailed development of independence in the female? I believe that the tendency of little girls to be less motorically impulsive, less physically aggressive, and less sexually active than little boys means that girls tend generally to get into less trouble than boys, tend not to engage in physical fighting, and tend not to masturbate. They are as a result less likely to perceive parents as people who thwart impulses. To the extent that girls are not separated from their parents as sources of support and nurturance, they are not forced to develop internal controls and an independent sense of self. In addition, girls can remain dependent and infantile longer than boys because the dependency, fears, and affection-seeking that are normal in early childhood for both sexes are defined as feminine in older children. Girls are, then, not pressed, by virtue of intense impulses, and by the culture's definition of "sissy" after the age of 2½, to become independent as early as boys. When the boy can no longer depend on continuous, nondemanding approval from his parents, he is pushed to develop internal, independent sources for good feelings about his self.

Unlike the boy, girls tend to continue in the affectionate, dependent relationships that are characteristic of all young children. More than boys, they will continue for an extended period of their lives to value the self as a function of reflected appraisals. This means, in a very pervasive and significant way, that unless something intervenes, the girl and then the woman will continue to have a great need for approval from others and that her behavior will be guided by a fear of rejection, or the fear of a loss of love. Although the prepubertal girl had a bisexual rearing in the sense that individual achievements, especially academic, were important resources for feelings of self-esteem, the emphasis changes at puberty. Our societal definition of successful femininity requires interpersonal success, especially with males; and at puberty the pressure on the girl increases to be successful in heterosexual relations. For the boy there is a parallel pressure to achieve esteem through individual academic or occupational successes.

What I am suggesting is that young girls are more dependent on others for feelings of self-esteem than boys are and that this dependency is increased at puberty because of our definition of femininity and successful role performance. The heterosexual relationship at puberty is clearly a sexual one, and anxiety and uncertainty about sex will increase the girl's vulnerability. The emotionally healthy daughter will tend to transfer her feelings of dependency, trust, and intimacy from her father to her boyfriend and then to her husband. But dependency implies vulnerability; although girls may become more sure of themselves and more independent, new relationships, especially with males, are likely to resurrect old needs, old fears, and a pressing search for reassurance. Even the healthy girl will be selectively dependent, especially in important emotional relationships and when she is not certain of her status within that relationship. Women perceive the world in interpersonal terms—that is, they personalize the objective world in a way that men do not. Notwithstanding occupational achievements, they regard themselves with esteem insofar as they are esteemed by those they love. Women remain dependent on the affectionate responses of their lovers, husbands, and children for good feelings about the self.

I think that young children perceive their sex as a verbal given or a label—one of the few things that they do not have to earn and that does not change as they grow older, as they succeed or fail, or as they are good or bad. Their sex identity remains a given until external demands make it something that has to be earned. At that time anxiety about one's sex, and therefore one's identity, begins. The pressure to become masculine, to grow up, to give up the femininity of childish behavior begins much earlier for boys than for girls, and sex identity may well be a crucial issue in the self-identity of the boy as early as the age of 5. Although the prepubertal girl anticipates her future role, I think that the crucial issues of feminine self-identity are postponed until the physical changes of puberty. At that time she will experience pressure to become really feminine and to inhibit masculine behaviors and personality traits. She will simultaneously experience pressure to succeed in heterosexual relationships and suffer restrictions on her freedom. Her sex identity, which now has to be proven, will fuse interpersonal success and adolescent perceptions of sex and reproduction.

Prepubertal girls are obviously aware of their sex: they practice certain housekeeping roles, they sometimes baby-sit, they mimic pregnancy with pillows, and they can tell you what their future responsibilities as women will be. But this is all just anticipatory play. When pubertal development results in the extraordinary physical changes of the menstrual cycle and the secondary sex characteristics, the girl's status will depend on her feminine desirability, and her psyche will depend on her acceptance of these happy and threatening changes. Now the source of her anxiety about her self-identity comes both from external pressures and from the radical changes within her own body. In adolescence and early adulthood, girls as well as boys are preoccupied with questions about their identity: their relations with others, their worth, their abilities, their goals, and their morality. For boys achievement is primary and affiliation is secondary; for girls the order of importance is reversed. Feminine sexual identity depends on heterosexual affiliative success. Affiliation is realistically perceived as the critical achievement for self-esteem, which, for a woman, depends on loving and being loved and respected by a man and then by one's children. Attitudes about the self and about the sexual self are critical.

I am going to suggest that in our middle-class culture the best that can be hoped for, in psychologically healthy girls, is an ambivalent attitude toward sex and reproduction. The psychological model of equal sexuality for boys and girls is not valid. The minimal masturbation observed in girls is not the result of massive repression but of the physiology of the female reproductive system. The girl has an insensitive vagina, no breasts, and a small and relatively inaccessible clitoris. Whereas male sexuality is always penile-genital and is a relatively linear development from childhood to adulthood, genital sexuality for girls occurs after puberty. Although prepubertal girls may be tactically sensitive, affectionate, and even sensual, they do not perceive the genitals as an important source of pleasure. This idea is important because it means that girls evolve their original concepts of sex and reproduction at a time when the genitals are not erotic or pleasurable.

It is strange but true that apparently negative feelings about menstruation and the menstruating woman are expressed in all cultures. The menstruating woman is labeled dirty, unclean, taboo. Advertisements for sanitary napkins and tampons assure the woman that, if she uses these products, she will be able to carry on as if she were "normal." The same negative affect surrounds the idea of pregnancy. We design maternity clothes to maximize the illusion of slenderness as long as possible, and we tell the pregnant woman that she, too, ought to carry on as though she were "normal." This situation implies that we view menstruating and pregnant women as abnormal. As a culture we deny the crisis qualities of menstruation, pregnancy, childbirth, and lactation; girls swiftly learn that these topics are not to be discussed (except, if they are lucky, in scientific terms in school) and that there is something "not normal" involved. As a result, they are given little opportunity to express their fears and gain reassurance.

For prepubertal girls, sex and sensuality—especially genital sex—are not highly salient topics. Girls anticipate having babies and being mothers, and they are curious; but I suspect that at best prepubertal girls view reproduction with ambivalence. While the child's tolerance for blood and pain is minimal, menstruation brings bleeding, the "curse," and the pain of cramps. Intercourse is intrusion into the most embarrassingly private part of the self. Pregnancy is awkward and distorted and culminates with the terror of labor. Lactation is something done by animals, especially cows. I sometimes think that penis envy or a general envy of males by adolescent girls stems from the fact that men do not menstruate or get pregnant.

Girls who have had no preparation for menstruation commonly express fears of having been ripped (or raped?) in their vulnerable body interior. Shainess (1961) found that even the 75% of the girls in her study group who did have advance information anticipated menstruation with anxiety, fear, and dread. Benedek (1959) writes that menstruation is the forerunner of the pain of defloration and of childbirth. Thus the girl's awareness of the uterus and the rest of the internal reproductive system emerges from pain and fear. Benedek continues by saying that the girl faces the enormous task of accepting the uterus and motherhood as part of her self; if she does so, she

Psychological conflict and the reproductive system

will be able to accept menstruation "without undue protest." This attitude is really very negative.

Menstruation is a critical event that arouses powerful and negative feelings about blood and pain as well as a narcissistic concern for the welfare of the body. The menstruating girl experiences periodic increases in sexual arousability and an increased anxiety about sex and mutilation. There is now a cycle of emotional changeability that also includes positive feelings of being normal and female. The girl feels grown up but is disappointed that her role in the world changes so little. She feels pleasure from the appearance of her body and from the sensuality of masturbation, but anxiety and guilt accompany that sensuality. In short, she is ambivalent.

With only one exception, every woman I have ever interviewed could recall the circumstances of her first menstrual period and how she felt about it. This fact alone attests to the enormous importance of the event in their lives. In a few rare cases young women I have interviewed considered menstruation a profound pleasure because it reassures their femininity. Most psychologically healthy American women whom I see simply report that menstruation is "just there," "all right," or "OK." What they mean is that it is not too intrusive in their lives.

I find it very interesting that in this culture emphasis and rewards are reserved for the cosmetic *exterior* of the sexual body—as though breasts and hips were created specifically for purposes of seduction. Adolescent girls can verbalize their concern about their competitive appearance but not their fears about internal reproductive functions. Defensively, fantasies about being torn or dismembered internally and ideas about blood, pain, and cruelty are submerged deeply into the unconscious. What we observe is a general irritation about having to menstruate that is only a dilute derivative of the original negative affect.

The healthy adolescent girl accepts her femininity, anticipates her sexual functions, takes pleasure in being desired and courted, and is acutely aware of the changes in her appearance. Because she is still responding to others, she values these physical changes primarily because they are a means of securing love. Her sexuality, emerging from pubertal changes, is confounded by fear and by her anticipation of love from the chosen. The adolescent crush is a very sexy relationship, but for the girl the sexuality involved is not vaginal. Although adolescent girls enjoy flirting, kissing, and petting, they are not motivated by strong genital urges. The adolescent girl fuses genital sexuality with maternity, she is not vaginally aroused, and she is afraid of becoming pregnant (although she is equally afraid of providing a contraceptive). Her primary motive for engaging in coitus is not the gratification of her own genital sexuality but the gratification of the needs of the male and the securing of his love.

The sexuality of the adolescent girl is combined with the rewards of dating. Dating is the testing ground for desirability as a woman, and the girl is ready to fall in love again and again because each relationship assures her of that desirability. She is much less aware of the sexual character of her feelings than is the boy; she enjoys the power of flirting but is very frightened that the boy will pressure her to intercourse. Characteristically she is ambivalent toward her genitals, simultaneously regarding them as something precious and as something dirty. The genitals are also a source of danger in our double-standard culture because participation in premarital coitus will lower her self-esteem in her own eyes and, even more dangerously, in the eyes of her lover. The girl's sexual inhibition has several origins: she is afraid of personal and social rejection; she has no intense, independent sex drive and thus has difficulty in perceiving vaginal sex as pleasurable; and she relates coitus to blood, mutilation, pain, penetration, and pregnancy. This combination of minimal vaginal eroticism, a frightened, masochistic view, and an internalized concept of a "good girl" will reinforce minimal sexuality. Girls are eager to grow up and enjoy the privileges of maturity, but they are frightened by the reality and responsibilities of their new body. Ambivalence toward the sexual body is likely to be a part of the psyche of most women. In addition, the girl, who is still evolving feelings of self-esteem, must be seductive enough to ensure dates and popularity but responsible enough to maintain control of sexual impulses.

The Need for Achievement in Sex. The infrequency of vaginal masturbation in young girls is probably not the result of massive repression so much as a derivative of the neural innervations of the vaginal barrel that make it relatively insensitive. Eroticism of the vagina does not normally occur until coitus. Moreover, because of the small size and inaccessibility of the clitoris, girls engage in relatively little clitoral masturbation.

Nevertheless, the periodic increase in sexual tension during the secretory or postovulation phase of the menstrual cycle, the increased erogeneity of the breasts, and the psychological concept of vaginal-penile fusion in coitus will combine in adolescence to create a demand for a metamorphosis from an asexual girl to a sexual woman.

I think that an important error has been made in much of the theory about female development. We have assumed that the vagina is like the penis and that the female hormone estrogen is like the male's testosterone—in effect, that female sexuality is the same as that of the male. We have made the achievement of an orgasm, preferably a "vaginal orgasm," a viable goal. What the data suggest is that girls are relatively asexual, that their sexual arousal not only takes more time but is more fragile or easily disturbed, and that there is a range of orgasmic reaction in females that is very different from the all-or-none phenomenon in males. We have viewed vaginal orgasm as identical to penile orgasm and as a necessary goal for both sexual partners. Yet the girl's sexual ambivalence, as well as her physiology, make this achievement difficult. The slower arousability of the female (despite the clitoris and skin erogeneity) and her infrequency of orgasm remind us that there is a difference in the imperativeness of sexual impulses in men and women. Sexual orgasm is a highly touted goal for women; but, in truth, I believe that love and maternity are far more crucial than sex in the woman's self-definition and self-esteem.

The orgasmic reaction of women includes a range of responses and is not limited to the single large response of men. Thus, although the reported frequency of orgasm in women includes lesser responses, it is still far lower than for men. Kinsey, Pomeroy, Martin, and Gebhard (1953) found that in their sample almost 100% of the boys but only 35% of the girls had achieved orgasm by the age of 17. Kinsey added that only 30% of the females reporting had achieved orgasm before marriage, and the maximum frequency after marriage was reached by age 35. (Experience and increased pelvic vascularity after pregnancy probably contribute to this rise in frequency.) Of interest is the work of Wallin (1960), who interviewed 540 wives. Some described themselves as rarely or never reaching orgasm but also reported that they usually experienced complete relief from sexual desires. This finding has two implications: (1) that intercourse as an affirmation of being loved is critical, and (2) that these women never reached high levels of sexual arousal in the first place. The orgasmic response depends on the level of sexual arousal; similarly, sexual frustration is a function of nongratification of a high level of arousal. Arousability is slower to develop in women than in men, and momentary levels of arousal tend to be lower. As a result, the excitement phase in women must be significantly longer than in men if they are to achieve a high enough plateau phase to reach orgasm (Masters & Johnson, 1966). The psychosomatic combination of infrequent masturbation, an insensitive vagina, an inaccessible clitoris, the absence of significant genital stimulation until middle or late adolescence, and the inhibitions resulting from ambivalence toward sex and the "good-girl" syndrome make arousal harder and customary levels of arousability lower. It is pathological when the male, having achieved an erection, is unable to achieve an orgasm. I think it is relatively uncommon when the female achieves sufficiently high arousal level that she experiences either frustration or a satisfying orgasm.

Many women whom I interview say that their sexual life is satisfactory although they never achieve an orgasm. And I believe them. They probably have never reached a sufficiently high level of arousal for the lack of an orgasm to result in discomfort or pain. Their only regret is the feeling that they are missing something that is supposed to be wonderful, and they feel rather cheated. Their disappointment is not a crucial problem. Another common response that I hear, especially with college-aged women, is that they do achieve orgasm and it is "pleasant." "Pleasant" does not describe a major orgasm.

I think it is fairly common for young and relatively inexperienced women to achieve a plateau state of arousal with relatively small and minor surges toward the orgasmic level. This kind of sensation is probably well described as pleasant or tingly. Maximal sexual arousal is not reached, a maximal orgasm is not achieved, resolution (the return to the pre-arousal state) occurs slowly, and there is a "nice" feeling without frustration. For these women the primary source of gratification is the feeling of loving someone and being loved. This kind of physical gratification can probably be achieved as well through petting as through coitus. Sex as the gratification of physical demands is subordinate to sex as an affectionate gratification. With some regrets but not deep grief, many women never leave this level of arousability.

That sex can be primarily a psychological rather than physi-

Psychological conflict and the reproductive system

cal act and therefore enjoyable without orgasm (even a minor one) clearly implies to me a lack of strong sexual arousal in the first place; the female who has reached a high plateau level of sexual arousal would need release from the physical tension created by that arousal or the experience would not be pleasant. Schaefer (1964) also found in her studies with women that orgasm is not always a factor in sexual contentment, that the orgasmic reaction appears to be learned rather than automatic, and that orgasm is experienced in an individual and subjective way.

The male model of a strong sexual drive is not generalizable to women. When physical impulses are not so powerful, the possibility for emotional contributions is stronger. Sexuality has a greater experiential component for women than for men, and it is more closely linked with emotional ties. The sexuality of the woman seems to me to be a developed ability. Through experience and experimentation, and in the trust of a stable, loving relationship, some women learn to maximize physical sensation and pleasure. They learn to forget the self, to discard old inhibitions, and to respond to the physical sensations of sexual arousal. The female who is sexually arousable has to be disinhibited, tactilly sensitive, psychologically able to give of herself, and capable of enjoying the awareness of body penetration. Women can be—and some are—spontaneously and honestly sensual; this capacity is just more uncommon in females than in males. The infrequency of high levels of arousal and orgasm contributes to the lack of strong sexual longings in women. Yet the expectation of high sexual responsivity as evidence of psychological health creates a physical and psychological need for successful sexual performance. The absence of a powerful sex motive in women is a logical extension of the anatomy of the female body and of the girl's relationship to her sexual body. The idea that women are motivated by strong sex drives has led to an overestimation of sex as a significant variable in their lives, an assumption of equal orgasmic responses, a failure to recognize the periodicity of desire as a function of menstrual endocrine changes, and an underestimation of the strength of maternity-nurturance needs. A large part of feminine sexuality has its origin in the need to feel loved, to feel reassured in that love, and to create love.

Sexual conflict arises from the assumption that the female must have an orgasm, which is the sign of successful sexual performance. Because she can participate in sex without being sexually aroused, she may feel debased, used, or prostituted. She may also feel anxious about her inability to become aroused and reach a vaginal orgasm. Masters and Johnson (1966) found that the vaginal orgasm is a fiction—the orgasm is a response of the entire pelvic area and the clitoris is always stimulated in any coital position. Sherfey (1966) has commented that women have difficulty in describing their sexual sensations, probably because they think they should experience something (that is, a vaginal orgasm) that they know they do not. Women are afraid that what they are feeling is not what healthy women should feel. This problem parallels the expectation that women respond simultaneously and similarly to men and the belief that the vagina is the site of important erogenous sensations. Coitus is the physical and psychological fusion with the loved man, but the site of sensations is not predominantly vaginal.

It is not surprising that, with few exceptions, the sexual life of women remains more inhibited than that of men. Simultaneously we have created a goal of fantastic sexual freedom and responsivity in women. In reality, women subordinate sexuality to maternity, deny the importance of orgasm and sexual arousal, and wonder whether what they feel is normal. Sex and pregnancy are intrusions into the self. The conditions for sexuality for girls are love and trust. Only in the romantic circumstances of mutual love and mutual commitment can the girl feel that she is not being used and that she is not desecrating her bodily integrity.

The Psychology of Sex and Unmarried Women. Mores about sex are evolving—they have not yet changed. Thus, although the incidence of premarital sexuality may be increasing, the older, internalized value judgments are still salient in the minds of the young, even if their behavior is at variance with those judgments. The cultural resexualization of the female body began only at the turn of the 20th century; yet already there has been a radical shift from the anticipated frigidity of the Victorian to the desired spontaneous sexuality of the Scandinavian. Despite the availability of inexpensive contraceptives with almost 100% effectiveness, we see premarital sex but not promiscuity. The responsibility for participating in sex still rests primarily with the girl. Whereas she may find it difficult to deliberately engage in premarital relationships (preferring a heady sweep of passion to override her inhibitions and defenses) because she is "good," she also feels pressure to engage in relationships to prove that she is not pathologically frigid or inhibited or square. The condition for sexual participation is the girl's perception of a mutual respect and commitment by both partners. But there is no certainty of commitment prior to the legalities of marriage, and participation in sex acts increases the girl's feeling of psychological vulnerability in the relationship. The "justification" for the sexual behavior is love, but ambivalence remains acute. In addition to the girl's ambivalence toward sex and her sexual body, she is also frightened by the idea that, by participating in premarital relationships, she has deprecated herself and will lose the male's respect and love. On the other hand, if she agrees to engage in premarital sex, the male is very likely to leave her. This possibility is not simply part of the mythology. Ehrmann (1959, p. 269) found that "males are more conservative and the females are more liberal in expressed personal codes of sex conduct and in actual behavior with lovers than with nonlovers. In other words, the degree of physical intimacy actually experienced or considered permissible is among males *inversely* related and among females *directly* related to the intensity of familiarity and affection in the male-female relation. . . ."

I think that, instead of proving to be the great liberator, absolute contraception has increased many girls' difficulties because it has removed the main realistic reason for virginity. Participating in sex and assuming the responsibility for contraception are important and conflict-ridden behaviors for most unmarried girls.

Zweben and I are presently conducting a study on the psychological consequences of taking oral contraceptives. Although this study was originally conceived of as a predictive study in psychosomatic responses to the Pill, it has actually turned out to be a study of the psychodynamics of sexual morality—probably because our 125 subjects are mostly young, unmarried college students.

Before the girls start to use the Pill, we give them a masculinity-femininity drawing test (the Franck), a passivity measure (Nichols), a detailed health questionnaire, and an hour-long standardized interview. Three months later we send them a detailed questionnaire and a four-picture TAT (Thematic Apperception Test). We do not know how typical our sample is. Our observations are similar to others reported in the literature, but it must be remembered that girls willing to participate in this study may represent an especially anxious population.

Psychosomatic response to the Pill seems to be a function of the strength of the motive to use it and of certain personality characteristics. Generally our subjects are extremely motivated not to get pregnant. The sample includes a few women who have had illegitimate children or abortions or who have close friends who have had these experiences.

An important variable in this study is denial, a psychological defense mechanism in which reality simply is not perceived. Women who are very passive and anxious sexually but who tend to use denial are reporting extraordinarily beneficent effects from the Pill: a decrease in menstrual-cycle symptoms such as premenstrual tension, an increase in sexuality and orgasmic reaction, and—rather amazingly—a loss of weight. Sex-anxious subjects who may be passive but do not use denial, and who have a history of menstrual-cycle symptoms or general hypochondriac tendencies, tend to report uncomfortable symptoms exactly the opposite of the positive effects just listed. Women who are not sexually anxious usually do not report physical symptoms. In other words, women who are not conflicted about sex do not regard the physical changes that occur with Pill use as symptoms. Women who are anxious about sex and who may be passive—who basically resent taking the Pill but use the defense mechanism of denial—perceive the physical changes as a reduction in symptoms. Those who are sexually anxious and who have a history of reacting to stress with a perception of symptoms in the reproductive system react to the Pill with an increase in symptoms.

Anxiety, guilt, and resentment about sex and about responsibility for contraception are revealed consciously by these girls' statements that they prefer to be responsible for contraception (even if there were something like a Pill for a man) because they cannot trust the men. On an unconscious level we find themes of abandonment and prostitution. Female eroticism in this sample is primarily psychological—a function of wanting to love someone or to secure love. Sex is justified only in the context of a love relationship, but our youthful subjects all tend to be anxious about their husbands or boyfriends. The majority of these young women are ambivalent about sex and have conflicted feelings toward their partners. Thus a not uncommon response on the follow-up questionnaire was that they felt more relaxed about sex. However, they also reported increased fatigue, decreased levels of sexual arousal, and a decrease in the frequency of orgasm.

When I asked these women why they made love, very few asserted that it was pleasurable for themselves. The healthier responses include ideas like "It makes us feel close" or "It's an expression of our love." Frequently I hear "It makes him happy," or "He wants it" or "It's expected." Few subjects report reaching orgasm, and yet they feel their sex life is satisfactory. They are consciously disappointed, but it is not terribly important. More significant to them is the feeling of closeness in the relationship that they ensure by their sexual participation.

But that attitude is also psychologically dangerous. When the sexual response is not mutual, and when sexual participation is motivated primarily to secure love in an uncertain relationship, the woman is giving herself. Whereas psychoanalysis talks about prostitution fantasies, we see in these young women prostitution anxieties. They feel that they have desecrated themselves in a nonfinancial, psychological form of prostitution because they have allowed themselves to be used in order to secure affection. Although we find this response in almost all our subjects, a premarital sexual relationship increases this psychological hazard. Without arousal the female is afraid of being used.

Thus, unconsciously, our subjects see themselves as prostituting themselves in the face of male demands that they go along with to avoid rejection. Women perceive themselves as being largely responsible for the success of interpersonal relationships. Their psychological vulnerability is maximized because their self-esteem is still dependent on others' acceptance of them, because they have a core fear of being rejected, because the heterosexual relationship is the most important achievement of their lives, and because they still define themselves in terms of relationships.

Unfortunately, we know that unmarried women often justify sex by a spontaneous and heady passion that dissolves all prior controls. (I say unfortunately because we see many of these girls in homes for unmarried mothers.) These girls do not use contraceptives, because having and using them represent forethought and the absence of this overwhelming spontaneous passion. It is clear that taking an oral contraceptive for

20 days out of every month is a conscious, deliberate, and repetitive act; it also becomes an anxiety-inducing act because it implies the conscious anticipation of sexual relations. Thus the use of the oral contraceptive is itself a significant behavior that increases anxiety and unconscious prostitution fears, with the result that the unmarried women in this study are even more fearful that men will hold them in contempt and abandon them.

Objectively, the use of the oral contraceptive can increase the woman's sexual freedom. It is therefore interesting to note that, although many subjects told me that they resent the male's greater freedoms, especially his sexual freedom, they never saw the Pill as giving them similar sexual license. At least in the subjects I have seen, conflict about the sexual use of the body has not diminished in spite of safe contraception and an evolving sexual freedom in this culture.

Psychosomatic Change in the Reproductive System

The woman's reproductive system can provide critically important feelings of self-esteem, and psychosomatic change in this salient system is often used as a psychological defense—that is, as a technique for keeping the personality intact. This system is an obvious and logical means by which women can express conflicts about aggression, anxiety, sexual feelings, maternity, and their relationships with themselves and other people. It is not accidental that certain women "choose" to wordlessly act out anxieties, fears, and hopes not only in general somatic symptoms but specifically and repetitively in the reproductive system. These symptoms express a strong conflict, which these women are unable to express more directly or resolve more efficiently.

Women who are very passive, dependent, sexually anxious, and prone to use the defense mechanism of denial are likely to express their conflicts through changes in the functioning of the reproductive system. Since the system is both psychologically salient and internal, it lends itself to such motivated dysfunctions. The working or not-working of this internal system seems automatic or nonvoluntary. Dysfunctions of this system are not guilt producing, and these women do not feel responsible for their symptoms.

Psychological conflict and the reproductive system

The passive, dependent, and conformist woman assesses the self by others' reactions to it. She is likely to tell an interviewer that she is independent and prides herself on that independence. This description not only is untrue but reflects her pervasive use of denial. The effects of denial are generalized: such women deny that their sex life is inadequate or unsatisfactory, they deny their general inadequacy, they deny their dependence, and they sometimes deny their femininity through a conversion symptom like amenorrhea. Because their behavior is motivated to fulfill others' expectations of what is normal, they express a conscious desire for sex, pregnancy, and maternity. However, these women often unconsciously reject their roles.

The psychological defense functions of psychosomatic symptoms are often very clear. For example, amenorrhea represents a denial of the menstrual flow and thus a regression to prepuberty, when dependency was normal and responsibility was minimal. This is also a regression to an asexual time and expresses sex anxiety. Amenorrhea symbolizes a denial of being an adult female and in reality prohibits conception. Sometimes the amenorrheic suppression of menstruation is a defense against sexuality and pregnancy, and sometimes it seems to be the denial of not being pregnant. The temporary amenorrhea of the unmarried girl may be a masochistic punishment for premarital sex or a sadomasochistic threat to force the male into marriage. Masochistic punishment may also appear as dysmenorrhea or traumatic vomiting in pregnancy. Other clinical syndromes affect the uterus and vagina, and they include habitual spontaneous abortion, premature labor, incoordinate uterine contractions, menstrual and menopausal tension, vaginismus, premature dilation of the cervix, premature rupture of the membranes, and pseudocyesis (false pregnancy) (Javert, 1957; Kelly, 1962).

The most elaborate of these syndromes is pseudocyesis, in which the symptom is a fusion of the wish and the fear. The body provides, in fantastic replication, the physical symptoms of the simultaneously feared and desired pregnancy. This pseudopregnancy is unconsciously motivated by the woman's desire to secure her husband's affection and give him a child, to prove her ability to conceive and be a successful woman, to achieve parity, and to effect masochistic self-punishment through the symptoms of pregnancy. In the fragility of her relationship with her husband, a real child would threaten the precarious balance. Thus pseudocyesis symbolically represents the needs, fears, and defenses of pathologically passive, dependent, insecure women.

I have characterized these women as very passive and dependent. Although dependency and passivity are normal characteristics of women, the generalization of these traits to all relationships and situations is abnormal. A woman whose self-esteem is so fragile that she cannot express hostility in any externalized form because she is afraid of the loss of love has little recourse but to behave nonaggressively in all situations with all people. Acting out one's anger and fears psychosomatically eliminates the need for overt aggression, but the symptom can effect a nonobvious aggression like denying a husband a child or invoking the fear of premarital pregnancy.

Because these women do not confront others directly with their fears and angers, they are able to effect a superficially good adjustment; they can still interact with people in a way that reduces the threatening quality of their anxieties, dependencies, and aggressions. These women alter the physical self in order not to jeopardize a relationship, since the breakup of that relationship would more seriously harm their self-esteem. But this defense is neither mature nor adaptive, and these women are unable to break out of the self-injurious pattern that they have defensively erected. Their ego controls tend to be infantile and their defenses primitive and vulnerable.

Passive, dependent women are characteristically ambivalent about being female and about the traditional feminine role responsibilities. They are unwilling to give up immature dependency satisfactions, especially from their husbands, and they defer to the males to secure affection. But simultaneously these women resent affectionate and role demands and see them as threats to their own dependency needs. It is obvious that a child represents an enormous threat because of the responsibility involved and because the husband may give love to the child. On the other hand, these immature, inadequate, and dependent women have few other resources for the development of self-esteem than success in the traditional responsibilities, which include sex and maternity. Thus it becomes necessary for them to perceive themselves as successful women who can master the traditional tasks. If they do not succeed in this area, their low self-esteem can only become more vulnerable. A psychosomatic conversion relieves one of responsibility: "I want to be pregnant. It's not my fault. I'm sick." And we always forgive the sick.

Behrman and I (Bardwick & Behrman, 1967) conducted an experiment that clearly revealed the motivated dynamics of psychosomatic conversion reactions in sexually anxious and passive women. We were studying changes in the contractions of the nonpregnant uterus, in response to sexual and nonsexual stimuli, at four different times in the menstrual cycle. Before the experiment, each of the ten very highly paid subjects (Ss) was given a psychological test battery. We found that we had accidentally selected two groups of Ss: Five were clearly passive and sexually anxious, four were neither passive nor sexually anxious, and one scored at the mean on the psychological measures (and later showed both kinds of uterine activity).

When they were confronted with the sexually relevant stimuli, the Ss who were sexually anxious, as compared to those who were not anxious, showed a greater increase in significantly deviant galvanic skin responses (GSR), basal-resistance-level responses, and uterine contractions. That is, the sexually anxious group was made more anxious by the sexual content of the stimuli than was the nonanxious group. Moreover, the sexually anxious Ss consistently gave a greater number of significantly deviant GSR and uterine responses to the sexual stimuli than they did to the nonsexual stimuli.

More interesting was the fact that the two groups of Ss displayed two distinctly different and consistent uterine patterns under arousal conditions. We measured uterine contractions by means of a small water-filled balloon that was inserted into the uterus. High-anxious Ss extruded the intrauterine balloon, and low-anxious Ss had uterine spasms. The Ss who were passive and sexually anxious extruded the intrauterine balloon into the vaginal tract without being aware of it. This response usually occurred when they were confronted with the sexual stimuli or shortly afterward. Extrusion was a consistent response—that is, it occurred during at least three of the four menstrual-cycle phases.

We interpreted the extrusion of the balloon as both a response to the experimental materials and an aggressive ending of the situation. The experiment came to an abrupt end, the anxiety situation ceased, and, although we did not have the desired data, Ss were still paid. Of course, these Ss were not aware that they had extruded the balloon until we told them.

One passive woman, who managed never to see the sexually relevant stimuli (after the first time), always abjectly apologized because the balloon was extruded and the data were incomplete and then remarked how angry she had been the *last time*. That is, her anxiety caused her to displace her anger to the past.

Under the same conditions the *S*s who were not passive or sexually anxious never extruded the intrauterine balloon. When these *S*s were most aroused, their uterine contractions consistently revealed brief uterine spasms superimposed on the basic large contractions. Other experiments have suggested that these muscle spasms might be the normal response of the uterus during coitus and could have the effect of increasing the probability of conception. The expulsive pattern of the anxious women would seem to have the opposite effect.

Affect Change and the Menstrual Cycle

Another kind of conflict in women that is also related to the reproductive system derives directly from the physiology of that system. Psychologists have traditionally studied body change or disease *resulting* from psychological states or motives, but now there is evidence that body change may also directly *affect* psychological states. Studies of the menstrual cycle reveal an extraordinary affect change in normal girls that correlates with menstrual-cycle phase. That is, at different cycle phases the personality is actually in conflict with itself. I am suggesting that there are regular and predictable changes in the personality of sexually mature women that correlate with changes in the menstrual cycle. These personality changes are extreme, they occur in spite of individual personality differences, and they are the result of the endocrine or other physical changes that occur during the cycle. The content of the change will be a function of the personality and real world of the individual, but the direction of the change will be a function of the physical state.

Reports of premenstrual depression, irritability, anxiety, and low self-esteem have varied in frequency from 25%–100% of the population, depending on definitions and types of measurement. Sutherland and Stewart (1965) studied 150 women and found that 69% of them experienced premenstrual irritability, 63% experienced depression, and 45% experienced both negative affects. Coppen and Kessel (1963), in their sample of 465 women, found that the levels of depression and irritability were more severe premenstrually than during menstruation. Although they felt that neurotic women may react more severely during the cycle phases, populations of normal, neurotic, and psychotic women show similar affect cycles. Similarly, Moos (1968) found that approximately 30%–50% of his sample of 839 women indicated, on a recall questionnaire, cyclic symptoms in irritability, mood swings, tension, or depression. (I strongly suspect that this result is an underestimate, because many women are unaware of these mood shifts. Affect change must be measured behaviorally—not through a questionnaire.)

These mood shifts are severe enough to affect behavior, and Dalton (1964) has found that a large proportion of the women who commit suicide or engage in criminal acts of violence do so during the premenstrual and menstrual phases of the cycle. She also found that, during the four premenstrual and four menstrual days, 45% of industrial employees reported sick, 46% of the psychiatric admissions occurred, 49% of the acute medical and surgical admissions occurred, 49% of prisoners committed their crimes, and 52% of the emergency admissions occurred. These data, along with the high frequency of symptoms in normal women, clearly suggest that this syndrome often has important consequences.

During the high-estrogen phase of ovulation, women experience high levels of self-esteem and low levels of negative affects. During the premenstrual phase, when the levels of the hormones estrogen and progesterone are low, there are strong feelings of helplessness, anxiety, hostility, and a yearning for love. Shainess (1961) found that the premenstrual phase was usually associated with these negative affects. Housman (1955) found an increasing need for affection and approval, a high sensitivity to interpersonal slight, and a high anxiety level during menstruation. Benedek (1959) has described the premenstrual phase as characterized by anxiety and depression, fears of mutilation and death, and sexual fantasies. She found that during ovulation there is almost a total absence of anxiety-related themes. Benedek and Rubenstein (1942) reported that, at the beginning of the menstrual cycle, when estrogen production is gradually increasing, there are good feelings of well-being and alertness; at ovulation the highest feeling of relaxation and well-being occurs; when the estrogen and progesterone levels swiftly decline during the premenstrual phase, there is a regression in the psychosexual integration. With some individual differences, premenstruation characteristically brings anger, excitability, fatigue, crankiness, crying spells, and a fear of mutilation. More than at any other time of the cycle, all emotions are less controlled, frustrations are perceived as unbearable, and the gratification of needs seems imperative. Benedek and Rubenstein found that the onset of menstruation was usually accompanied by a relaxation of the tension and irritability, although this relief was often mixed with a feeling of depression that continued until estrogen production increased.

I would like to illustrate the enormity of the psychological changes that occur even in normal subjects. Ivey and I (Ivey & Bardwick, 1968) studied a group of 26 normal college students over two menstrual cycles. Twice at ovulation and twice at premenstruation they were asked to tell us about some experience they had had. These verbal samples were tape-recorded and were later scored using Gottschalk's Verbal Anxiety Scale (Gottschalk, Springer, & Gleser, 1961). We scored Death, Mutilation, Separation, Guilt, Shame, and Diffuse Anxiety. The premenstrual anxiety scores were significantly higher (at the 0.0005 level) * than the anxiety scores at ovulation.

When we combined the scores for all the subjects, we found that the Death Anxiety score at premenstruation was significantly higher than that at ovulation ($p < 0.02$), as was the Diffuse Anxiety score ($p < 0.01$). Separation Anxiety, Mutilation Anxiety, and Shame Anxiety were also higher premenstrually (at approximately 0.13 levels), whereas Guilt Anxiety remained fairly constant.

Because the instructions were nonexplicit and simply asked the subject to talk about some experience, the shifts in content become important. When we examined the verbal samples for consistent topics, we found recurring themes that were unique to a menstrual-cycle phase. A constant theme at ovulation was self-satisfaction over success or the ability to cope:

> . . . so I was elected chairman. I had to establish with them the fact that I knew what I was doing. I remember one particularly problematic meeting, and afterward, L. came up to me and said, "you really handled the meeting well." In the end it came out the sort of thing that really bolstered my confidence in myself.

* That is, the odds that this effect could occur by chance are 5 in 10,000.

The following sample came from the same girl premenstrually during the same cycle:

> They had to teach me how to water-ski. I was so clumsy it was really embarrassing, 'cause it was kind of like saying to yourself you can't do it and the people were about to lose patience with me.

Another theme that occurred often was hostility. The following response was recorded at premenstruation:

> ... talk about my brother and his wife. I hated her. I just couldn't stand her. I couldn't stand her mother. I used to do terrible things to separate them.

This angry and incestuous verbal sample is in striking contrast to the same girl's sample from the ovulatory phase of the same cycle.

> Talk about my trip to Europe! It was just the greatest summer of my life. We met all kinds of terrific people everywhere we went and just the most terrific things happened.

The theme of Death Anxiety was evident at premenstruation:

> I'll tell you about the death of my poor dog. . . . Oh, another memorable event—my grandparents died in a plane crash. That was my first contact with death, and it was very traumatic for me. . . . Then my other grandfather died.

In contrast, the sample at ovulation for the same girl was as follows:

> Well, we just went to Jamaica and it was fantastic. The island is so lush and green and the water is so blue. . . . The place is so fertile and the natives are just so friendly.

My last example is an illustration of premenstrual Mutilation Anxiety, which was in strong contrast to the contented ovulation narrative for the same girl during one cycle:

> ... we came around a curve and did a double flip and landed upside down. I remember the car coming down on my hand and slicing it right open, and all this blood was all over the place. Later they thought it was broken because every time I touched the finger it felt like a nail was going through my hand.

At ovulation she told of the following experience:

> We took our skis and packed them on top of the car, and then we took off for up North. We used to go for long walks in the snow and it was just really great—really quiet and peaceful.

Studies in which the menstrual cycle is the independent variable are confounded by the subjects' awareness of the experimenters' interest in the cycle phases. However, we had one unexpected and accidental experimental control. One girl was interviewed on the fourteenth day of her menstrual cycle, and the verbal sample was almost twice as anxious as the ovulation sample of the previous menstrual cycle. Thematically, there were references to death, mutilation, and separation. The next day she began to menstruate—two weeks early.

An extension of this study by my student Paige and me (Paige, 1969) not only has replicated these results but provides further support for the idea that the mood state is a function of the physiological state. We hypothesized that, if the levels of anxiety and hostility expressed in the verbal samples are related to the levels of estrogen and progesterone, then women who use oral contraceptives should be different from women who do not use them. For women using the Combination Pill (which provides a constant amount of these hormones for 20 days), we predicted that the relatively constant level of these hormones would eliminate the cyclic fluctuations in moods. For women not using the Pill and for those using the Sequential Pill (which provides a hormone cycle simulating that of normal menstruating women), we predicted that the level of anxiety and hostility would again be lowest at ovulation and highest at premenstruation.

Paige, using the Gottschalk Scales, analyzed the verbal samples of 102 married women, collected at four times during the menstrual cycle. There were three groups of subjects: one group of 38 women who were not using oral contraceptives and never had; a second group of 52 women who were using the

Combination Pill (20 consecutive days of tablets containing both estrogen and progestin, followed by approximately 7 days without the Pill); and a third group of 12 women who were using the Sequential Pill (15 consecutive days of tablets containing only estrogen, followed by 5 days of tablets containing both estrogen and progestin, followed by approximately 7 days without the Pill).

We again found that the cycle phase had a very significant effect on the anxiety and hostility levels of women who were not using the Pill. (Analysis of variance results were: hostility $= p < 0.001$; anxiety $= p < 0.05$). As we had hypothesized, the changes in the levels of anxiety for women taking Sequential Pills followed the same pattern as those for non-Pill users. For women taking Combination Pills, the cycle phase had no significant effect on their levels of hostility or anxiety (hostility $= p < 0.95$; anxiety $= p < 0.25$).

Therefore the cyclic change in affects that was found in the first study was replicated in the second for menstruating non-Pill users and for women whose contraceptives follow the normal endocrine pattern. Women who use the more common Combination Pill—who have constant high levels of estrogen and progestin—do not experience the same wide swings in affects. When the hormone level is rather constant, as in the case of women taking Combination Pills, anxiety and hostility levels are correspondingly constant. When the endocrines fluctuate during the menstrual cycle, corresponding fluctuations occur in emotions.

Thus these physical (especially endocrine) changes so influence psychological behavior that, despite personality differences, and even in normal women, psychological behavior becomes predictable on the basis of menstrual-cycle phase. These data suggest that physical states, as well as core psychological characteristics, will determine whether women will cope or not cope; will be anxious, hostile, or depressed when tested; or will appear healthy or neurotic on psychological tests.

The reproductive system of women is the most salient physical system for the gratification of needs for self-esteem and for the expression of needs, affects, and conflicts. It is also a system that directly affects these psychological variables. Menstruation, pregnancy, childbirth, lactation, and menopause are all periods of normal crisis for women and should be understood as such.

References

Bardwick, J. M., & Behrman, S. J. Investigation into the effects of anxiety, sexual arousal, and menstrual cycle phase on uterine contractions. *Psychosomatic Medicine,* 1967, **29**(5), 468–482.

Bardwick, J. M., & Zweben, J. E. A predictive study of psychological and psychosomatic changes associated with oral contraceptives. In preparation.

Benedek, T. Sexual functions in women and their disturbance. In S. Arieti (Ed.), *American handbook of psychiatry.* New York: Basic Books, 1959. P. 726.

Benedek, T., & Rubenstein, B. *The sexual cycle in women: The relation between ovarian function and psychodynamic processes.* Washington, D. C.: National Research Council, 1942.

Coppen, A., & Kessel, N. Menstruation and personality. *British Journal of Psychiatry,* 1963, **109**, 711–721.

Dalton, K. *The premenstrual syndrome.* Springfield, Ill.: Thomas, 1964.

Ehrmann, W. *Premarital dating behavior.* New York: Holt, 1959.

Gottschalk, L. A., Springer, K. J., & Gleser, G. C. Experiments with a method of assessing the variations in intensity of certain psychological states occurring during two psychotherapeutic interviews. In L. A. Gottschalk (Ed.), *Comparative psycholinguistic analysis of two psychotherapeutic interviews.* New York: International Universities Press, 1961. Chap. 7.

Housman, H. A psychological study of menstruation. Unpublished doctoral dissertation, University of Michigan, 1955.

Ivey, M. E., & Bardwick, J. M. Patterns of affective fluctuation in the menstrual cycle. *Psychosomatic Medicine,* 1968, **30**(3), 336–345.

Javert, C. *Spontaneous and habitual abortion.* New York: McGraw-Hill, 1957. Chap. 12.

Kelly, J. V. Effects of fear upon uterine motility. *American Journal of Obstetrics and Gynecology,* 1962, **83**(5), 576–581.

Kinsey, A. C., Pomeroy, W. B., Martin, C. E., & Gebhard, P. H. *Sexual behavior in the human female.* Philadelphia: Saunders, 1953.

Masters, W. H., & Johnson, V. E. *Human sexual response.* Boston: Little, Brown, 1966.

Moos, R. H. The development of a menstrual distress questionnaire. *Psychosomatic Medicine,* 1968, **6**, 853–867.

Paige, K. E. The effects of oral contraceptives on affective fluctuations associated with the menstrual cycle. Unpublished doctoral dissertation, University of Michigan, 1969.

Schaefer, L. Sexual experiences and reactions of 30 women. Unpublished doctoral dissertation, Columbia University, 1964.

Shainess, N. A re-evaluation of some aspects of femininity through a study of menstruation: A preliminary report. *Comprehensive Psychiatry,* 1961, **2,** 20–26.

Sherfey, M. J. The evolution and nature of female sexuality in relation to psychoanalytic theory. *Journal of the American Psychoanalytic Association,* 1966, **14**(1), 28–128.

Sutherland, H., & Stewart, I. A critical analysis of the premenstrual syndrome. *Lancet,* 1965, **1,** 1180–1183.

Wallin, P. A study of orgasm as a condition of woman's enjoyment of intercourse. *Journal of Social Psychology,* 1960, **51,** 191–198.

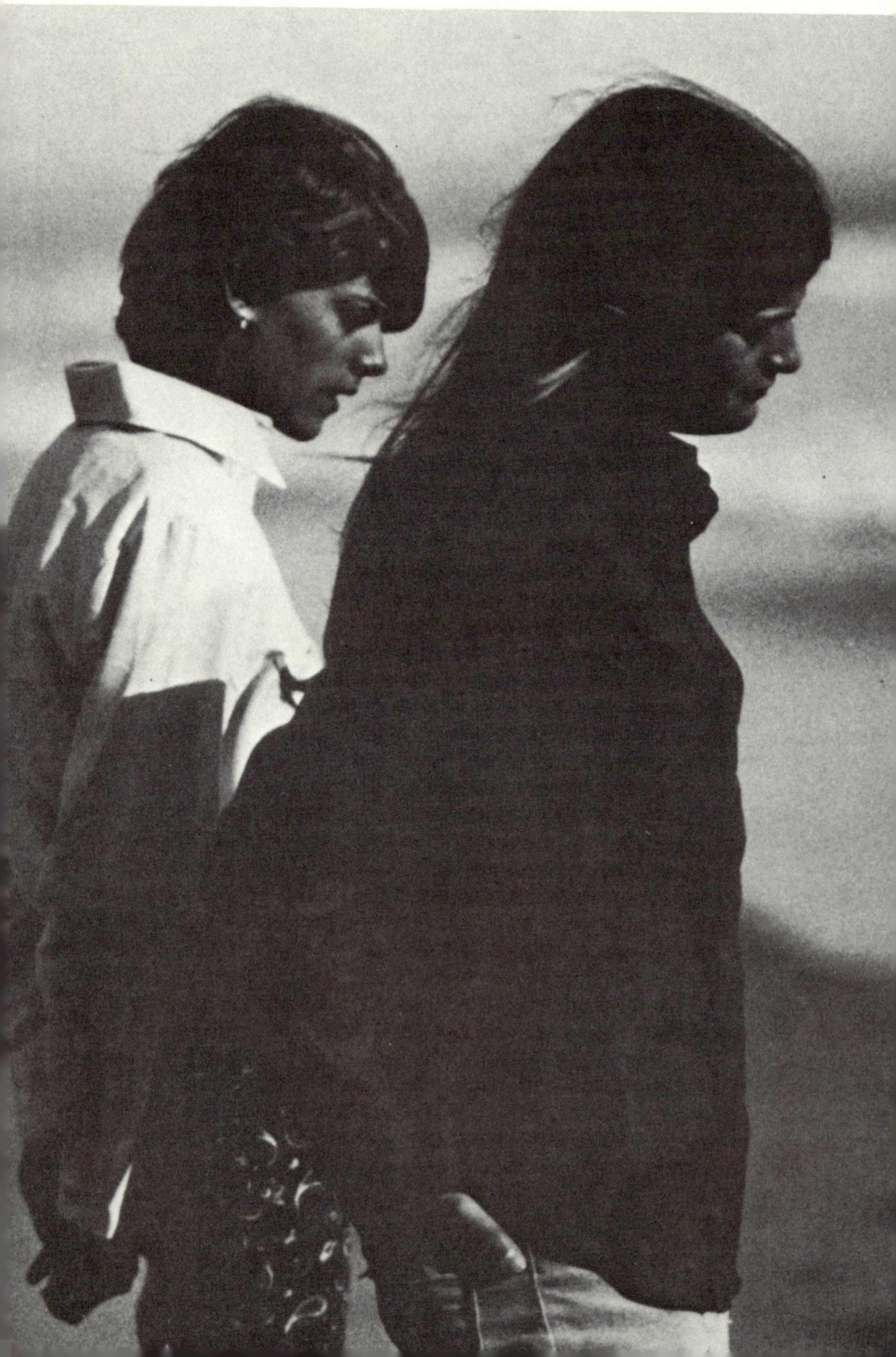

2

new sources of conflict in females at adolescence and early adulthood

Elizabeth Douvan

Psychologists have looked at the changes of puberty in much the same way that we look at someone else's troubles: We muse over them, stand awed by their enormity, perhaps gasp with relief that they are not ours, and then usher them out of our consciousness. Awe may contribute to our sympathy and admiration for beleaguered friends, but in science it inhibits rational analysis. Our understanding of pubertal changes reflects the influence of such awe. We have some careful descriptions of the physiological developments of puberty but almost no significant studies of the way in which these developments are mediated into the psychic life of the child. The one area that has been rather thoroughly studied is developmental pacing: the advanced sexual development of girls (approximately one year earlier than that of boys) has been tied to certain features of female psychic development that are also about one year advanced. The pacing issue has also been considered within sex groups: psychic effects of early and late maturation in boys have been explored in a series of exceptionally fine studies by Mussen and Boutourline-Young (1964). Stone and Barker made the classic, although more limited, study of the effects of pacing on girls (1937, 1939).

Content differences in the developmental process experienced by boys and girls have not been closely attended to, and they seem to me to offer important testable ideas about psychological development. I will first concentrate on some hypotheses drawn directly from the content of physiological changes and then briefly analyze some interpersonal and cultural complications that have particular relevance for the girl's development at adolescence.

To begin with physiological issues, let us look at the menarche and its broad implications. We know from ethnographies that menstruation is viewed by various societies as illness, as a period of particular fragility and vulnerability, as a powerful magical contamination, and as a condition dangerous enough to require physical isolation (Mead, 1949). But what is menstruation on the physiological and psychological levels? It is the beginning of emphatic periodicity in the girl's life—the starting of regular hormonal changes that we know are influential in mood states, in emotionality and its management, in general body tone, in water retention by body tissue, and in other physiological and psychic conditions. The menarche introduces the peculiarly female condition in which the whole body system is subject to regular periodic transformation—a condition unlike any of the equally significant changes a boy experiences at puberty.

I would like to suggest that this regular fluctuation in the body system—unique in the phenomena of normal physiology—adds special conflicts to the already problem-ridden process of developing a stable self-concept at adolescence. It will, I think, alter both the process and the final outcome of the adolescent search for self. Specifically, it will result in a self-system that is more fluid and more vulnerable to environmental influences than the self-system developed by boys.

Discovering the self is a significant part of the adolescent task that Erikson (1950) has highlighted and labeled the "quest for identity." All theories of adolescence recognize it in one form or another as one of the central problems for youngsters between puberty and adulthood, and all agree that the changes of puberty initiate the quest and that radical pubertal body changes both stimulate and endanger the process of self-discovery. Here is the young person—testing and investing identifications, talents, and skills that he brings from his past; selecting among roles offered by his society, and making an effort to join these inner and outer realities in a personal integration that is both comfortable for him and legitimate in the eyes of those significant others to whom he looks for self-confirmation. The changes of puberty stimulate the process; for example, developing genital capacity requires mastery and inclusion in the self-concept. Yet the integrative task is enormously complicated by the fact that the most familiar of all realities, the body itself, is changing in all dimensions and functions at a startlingly brisk pace. How can an adolescent be sure who he is when his body grows six inches in a year and presents new and puzzling impulses? On reflection it seems remarkable that adolescence proceeds for most youngsters with so few, rather than so many, problems.

Although the pubertal changes that the boy experiences are radical and complicate his identity problem, they are at least unidirectional. His frame enlarges, his voice deepens, and his glandular functions and sexual interests quicken. But, once changed, they can again become familiar realities, for the changes occur only once. For the girl, however, certain changes occur and then recur each month, and they are specifically changes in affect states that are likely to touch on feelings about the self. Since internal cues vary widely and appear unstable, the girl will come to rely more heavily than the normal boy on external cues and the expectations of significant others—on feedback from an audience—as anchors for her self-definition.

Perhaps if girls clearly and consciously connected changes in their feeling states to the fact of menstruation, they could at least isolate the feelings associated with premenstrual tension and define them out of the self-concept. They could say: "I am not myself at this point. Since I am about to menstruate and am powerfully affected by changes in my body system, this behavior is not part of the self that is really me." But it is my impression, from both personal and clinical conversations, that this level of consciousness of body functions and of the connection between mood shifts and the menstrual cycle is uncommon and almost exclusively found in women who have experienced pregnancy, childbirth, and the dramatic emotional accompaniments of these physiological events. Ivey and Bardwick (1968) found radical shifts in affect accompanying premenstrual hormonal changes in 23 out of 26 normal girls. Yet in most samples of high school and college girls we find repeatedly that only about 10% recognize such shifts in mood as related to the menstrual cycle (Douvan & Kaye, 1956; Tangri, 1969; Gold & Williams, 1969). This combination of findings suggests that the changes are not under very adequate ego control. A great deal of clinical evidence attests to the ease with which not only mood changes, but the whole fact of

New sources of conflict in females at adolescence and early adulthood

menstruation, can be denied or split off from consciousness (see, for example, Deutsch, 1945; for a summary of gynecological reports on this issue, see Bardwick, 1970).

The menstrual cycle is outstanding among somatic functions in its vulnerability to psychic factors. Dysmenorrhea is commonly regarded by experienced gynecologists as a psychosomatic complaint. Menstruation is also susceptible to denial. Many cases in the clinical literature support the hypothesis that amenorrhea and irregularity in menstruation are symptoms of a basic rejection of femininity. Treatment of the psychological problem predictably relieves the somatic symptom.

I have suggested that periodicity disrupts the girl's developing self-concept and that the cyclic character of internal cues makes her depend on external information for self-direction. There is some evidence to support this idea in Witkin's (1954) work on field dependence. This research used a variety of techniques but can be typified by the rod-and-frame task. A projected lighted frame is presented to subjects (Ss), who are asked to adjust a movable rod within the framed space to an upright position. Since the frame is also movable and can be varied around the upright stance, the test provides a measure of the S's reliance on or independence from external cues (the frame) for establishing an upright rod. The most reliable difference in all of Witkin's studies is a sex difference: Women consistently depend more on external cues and less on self-generated internal cues in judging space orientation. However, this sex difference does not appear in studies of children. It first becomes obvious at the age of 10 or 11—just about the time of the menarche. The girl becomes more dependent on context cues and more sensitive to her surroundings. I would suggest, then, that the periodic disruption in the body systems through the menstrual cycle has unsettled the girl's clarity about herself, imposed more complex demands for ego synthesis, and cast doubt on the reliability of internal cues. The girl orients toward external cues because the nature of her internal cues is not so certain or stable. I would like to see someone repeat Witkin's work but tie these developments to measures of physiological development rather than chronological age. Nevertheless, at this point the findings are at least provocative.

The girl at puberty is confronted by a sexual development that is inherently more ambiguous and diffuse than that of the boy. The one clear external mark of sexual development in the girl is menstruation. Her sexual and reproductive organs are internal and inaccessible, and her sexual excitation creates no dramatic external changes comparable to erection and ejaculation. Female sexuality is a more diffuse physiological response, its excitation requires more specific stimulation than the male sex drive, and, finally, it is not associated with a visible body organ. Genital sexual impulses are new to the boy at adolescence; but they are quite specific and imperious, and they center in a familiar body organ that has been a source of pleasure to him since his phallic period at 4 or 5. The boy may have much to learn before he will realize full sexual expression, but the drive is explicit and the organ system known (Douvan, 1960).

The greater ambiguity of the girl's developing sexuality is at least one factor underlying special features of her interpersonal development at adolescence. For example, it may account for the importance and special qualities of close, like-sexed friendships among girls. The special intensity, mutuality, and sharing that girls seek and find in friendship (and that distinguish their friendships from the more activity-centered, less intimate colleagueships of boys) may stem from the girl's need to discover the nature and meaning of her sexual impulses by sharing information and feelings with other girls who are experiencing the same mysterious and unsettling new impulses.

I have found through interviews that girls at about the age of 14—who have recently undergone pubertal changes and are beginning heterosexual dating—are most likely to stress the sharing of intimacies in their definitions of friendship and to be particularly sensitive to the issue of security-loyalty in the relationship. If, as I suspect, the sharing centers on sexual knowledge and sexual secrets, it is not surprising that loyalty becomes a critical concern: A disaffected friend may carry away with her some highly dangerous knowledge!

For girls the like-sexed friendship has and maintains a greater importance than boy-girl relationships throughout the adolescent period. Moreover, these like-sexed friendships develop an intimacy and maturity that are not found in boys' like-sexed peer relations. Whereas boys look to the peer group for support in their strike for independence, girls use the peer group to find a close friend. A boy becomes a man by breaking out of the family circle, and he uses the peer group toward this end. The girl, without giving up her dependent relationship to

New sources of conflict in females at adolescence and early adulthood

the family, develops much more intimate friendships than the boy does. This difference in social development may result from the difference in sexual development in the two sexes. Biological sexuality is stated directly and forcefully for the boy. His task is to leave the family circle (with its incestuous dangers) and find relationships within which he can express and gratify the sex drive without danger. The girl's more ambiguous sexuality requires exploration and definition, and the close like-sexed friendship provides a safe haven within which girls can talk about and clarify the nature and normality of their developing sexual selves (Douvan & Adelson, 1966; Douvan, 1960).

The inherent ambiguity of the female sex drive has other consequences. In studies of sexual expression, one finding is ubiquitous: girls' sexual expression, in behavior or fantasy, is significantly lower than boys'. Kinsey's data are clear on behavioral expression over several generations and cultures. Samples for females report a lower incidence of all forms of overt sexual expression (masturbation, petting, coitus) than for males and a higher average age at which first experiences occur (Kinsey, Pomeroy, Martin et al., 1948; Asayama, 1957).

Since cultural standards are so imposing regarding sexual behavior, the data on fantasy are even more interesting. Kinsey's data are again helpful: females report many fewer sexual dreams than males, and the difference is particularly large during adolescence (Kinsey et al., 1953).

Using stories collected in response to Thematic Apperception Test (TAT) pictures (Murray et al., 1943), both Symonds (1949) and Sanford et al. (1943) found that, at puberty, boys' stories show a dramatic increase in sexual themes but girls' stories show a decrease in such themes. This finding gains significance from the fact that aggressive themes rise sharply at puberty for both sexes. How can we explain the decrease in girls' sexual fantasy? We might concede that boys' sexual impulses are stronger than girls' and that boys will therefore show a larger increase in sexual fantasy (even though they have greater access to direct expression). But we cannot in any event reasonably entertain the idea that the sex drive of girls *decreases* at puberty. Some more complicated explanation must be sought, and the same data offer a clue to its nature. Girls' stories show an increase in themes of abasement at puberty—that is, in themes of self-damage and self-disparagement. Moreover, the curves for sexual themes and abasement themes are neat mirror images of each other: When sexual themes decrease, abasement themes increase, and vice versa. At puberty girls do not express intensified sexual impulses through overt behavior or fantasy, but they show signs of increased anxiety and defensiveness.

It is probably true that cultural standards contribute to this differential reception of genital sexuality in boys and girls; however, it seems to me that we should look closely at the events of that development as it occurs in the two sexes before we look for cultural explanations. Genital maturity in girls is marked most obviously by the menarche, a development that lends itself to mixed and primitive fantasy. Associated with hurts and wounds and body waste, it is the essence of primary process—the vivid, concrete, imagistic, prelogical thought process shared by dreams and poetry. Despite calm, scientific, maternal explanations, this central mark of the girl's impending adulthood is well designed to induce anxiety. Add to this the fact that the crucial pubertal changes are internal and inaccessible, and the stage is set for the anxious and defensive response that we observe in girls.

Anxiety about physiological developments spreads to the interpersonal sphere, where it influences and conditions the nature of relationships and conflicts that arise in those relationships. The internal and indefinite quality of the girl's sexuality makes her particularly dependent on relationships with other girls. In the process of sharing experiences, information, feelings, and wisdom with her girlfriends, the young girl comes to a clearer apprehension—if not a refined understanding—of her sexual nature. The cyclic quality of her emotions and moods probably also affects the stability of her relationships: We know that friendships at this life stage are highly unstable (Horrocks & Thompson, 1946; Thompson & Horrocks, 1947). The data by Ivey and Bardwick (1968) on premenstrual depression and the acting out of premenstrual aggressive impulses (that is, the tendency to behave aggressively rather than check the impulse at a symbolic level) make it seem remarkable that girls salvage any stable relationships at all.

The adolescent girl faces a new source of interpersonal conflict in the institution of dating. Early dating among American adolescents is an almost pure example of what sociologists call a role relationship. It is narrowly restricted and governed almost completely by normative prescriptions and expectations. Manners and dress are dictated by norms, but so are

New sources of conflict in females at adolescence and early adulthood

nuances of style and mood. A good date is cheerful, easy in conversation, a good listener, neither too aggressive nor too passive, and never grouchy, moody, or too sexual. The dating personality is a codified system known to girls in early and middle adolescence (Douvan & Adelson, 1966) and promulgated by the teen columns and magazines. The dating system and competition for dates create new conflicts for the girl:

1. She becomes pressed to develop and concentrate on the most external, superficial aspects of the self at a time when the inner demand for self-definition is equally pressing. The sense of continuity that Erikson (1950) puts at the center of the identity task—the feeling of self-sameness and identity between what one is and what one seems to be—is specifically obstructed by involvement in the dating ritual. The girl may either separate the two aspects of the self or lose track entirely of the inner self under the pressure to attract affection and attention.
2. Dating expands the discrepancy between the self "as I really am" and the self "as others see me." It further fragments the self by prescribing interactive styles in dating that are alien and inappropriate to like-sexed friendships. The girl then distinguishes the self as it relates to boys from the self as it relates to other girls. Competition for dates and for boyfriends raises a problem of ethics in friendships: the conflict between loyalty-solidarity and competitiveness. The girl must somehow resolve the problem of defining priorities and allocating commitments—to herself, to her desire for popularity and attention, and to the claims of friendship.

Some of the conflicts raised by physiological developments and by interaction with peers are picked up and exaggerated for the girl by the broader culture and its definitions of adult sex roles. Certainly the culture supports the pubertal girl's field dependence, which lies at the core of the traditional definition of the feminine role. The girl is encouraged to remain fluid and ambiguous in self-definition and to orient toward an external audience for a reflected sense of self, for cues in making judgments, and for the acceptance that will anchor her self-esteem.

The culture's norms regarding sex-appropriate behavior also bear in and make their mark at adolescence. The child's sexual maturation stimulates new pressure from adults charged with his socialization (primarily but not exclusively his parents).

Adults are likely to see adolescence as a last chance to influence the child and, as such, a very important and serious challenge. Whatever settlements adolescents work out in crucial areas like sex-role performance are taken seriously by concerned adults, because they are seen as permanent settlements. The games of childhood suddenly take on the serious quality of being "for keeps." Little boys can indulge a taste for sewing or housework without causing great alarm. If a little boy has long hair, he is assumed to be either too poor to afford a barber or the son of fashionable Anglophiles. But if he continues to wear his hair long in junior high and high school, many parents react with an intensity that signals primitive fear. They are afraid that the boy about to become an adult is choosing a deviant course in this most crucial and primitive area of identity—alignment with his own sex group.

Sexual maturation makes the adolescent the target of intensified pressures from the culture, and that same maturation leaves him especially vulnerable to outside pressure because it disrupts his previously workable impulse-defense balance. He has little confidence in his own ability to manage his new impulses and therefore relies on the directives that are so anxiously offered by parents and other adults. Evidence from the Fels Research Institute's longitudinal studies indicates that adolescence is the time when youngsters abandon characteristics that are inappropriate to their sex group. Kagan and Moss (1962) found that, at about puberty, boys abandon, deny, or sublimate dependency and girls give up overt aggressiveness. Analysis of sex-role prescriptions has led Kagan (1964) to conclude that the girl is especially vulnerable to social pressure. He points to the fact that the boy's masculine self-concept is based at least in part on skills that are measurable and pleasurable aside from social feedback (such as scoring hits on a basketball backboard) but that the girl's self-concept is almost entirely dependent on social skills that can be measured or proven only by the response of an audience.

Coleman's (1961) study of high school students revealed the impress of sex-role definitions on the value system of the adolescent peer culture. Athletic interest for boys and popularity for girls are the values stressed and approved by the peer group. Coleman's findings also indicate that the sex-linked goal of social facility and popularity is a highly concentrated system that maintains its dominance for girls throughout high school and often obstructs the development of other values, such as

New sources of conflict in females at adolescence and early adulthood

academic achievement. As boys move through the high school years, academic values take on increasing importance for them (although they never actually overtake the values of athletic skill and athletic-mindedness). But for girls, academic values continue to decline in importance throughout the high school period, and popularity and social leadership maintain their ascendance. The same emphasis continues for most girls beyond high school, even in the academically select population of students in Eastern women's colleges and under the special achievement pressure that college represents.

In the Vassar studies (Sanford et al., 1956) and in Newcomb's (1943) studies at Bennington, the social theme challenged academic values for the majority of girls. Sizable groups in both populations (from one-fourth to one-third of the total) were distinctly more interested in popularity, affable peer relationships, and social leadership than in academic subjects or intellectual achievement of any kind.

The broader culture, like the peer culture, reinforces an outward turn just when the girl's physiology is pressing her to turn in—to integrate newly proliferated feelings and facets of the self. Adolescence is, after all, the age of self-exploration. Heightened narcissism is as prominent as selflessness. Adolescence is the age of diary-keeping, which is primarily a feminine expressive form. In questioning undergraduate students over the last several years, I have found that many more girls than boys have kept diaries during adolescence (more than 50% of the 200 girls questioned, compared to 8% of a group of 200 boys). Boys write more narrative fiction (adventure stories like Penrod's tales of Harold Ramorez), which functions to externalize and objectify impulses rather than to explore them. Those boys who have written diaries use them for objective and short-term purposes: The boy's diary is either a log (tied to a trip or other specific adventure) or a means for coming to terms with a specific externally induced problem. The intense exploration and integration of internal events that characterize the girl's use of the form are conspicuously absent in the boy's.

Feminine Personality & Conflict

Thus girls are concerned with self-discovery, although not necessarily in specific vocational terms and with much less emphasis on individual achievement than boys show. Nevertheless, they are equally eager to discover those special gifts and competencies that all adolescents need to build self-esteem

(Friedenberg, 1959). Their competence is not necessarily limited to the interpersonal sphere.

The outward turn urged on the girl by the culture does not always lead to conflict. Many of the skills and sensitivities encouraged by this constant orientation to an audience are probably useful to her later in performing her adult roles of wife and mother. Moreover, her attention to charm and the winning of affection serves an important defensive function in that it forestalls anxiety about whether she will in fact be chosen in marriage. But, for most women, popularity and social charm will not sustain self-esteem for a lifetime, and it seems to me that we miss an important opportunity to help the girl enlarge her self-concept when we fail to capture and turn the ferment of adolescence to this purpose. Because we fear aggressiveness in women, we push the girl to disavow all internal anchors for self-definition. We encourage her to remain tentative in self-outline so that she may adapt more easily to the man she marries and so that she does not develop herself out of any part of the market of potential husbands.

Because American culture overspecializes its sex-role prescriptions for adolescents—narrow vocationalism for boys and winning charm as marriage insurance for girls—it is no accident that the youth protest has focused so deliberately on these issues. While boy hippies refuse to join the rat race (that is, the masculine world of work), girl hippies refuse to wash their hair and seem, rather, intent on washing out all external signs of feminine attractiveness.

David Gutmann's provocative chapter in this book (Chapter 4) will deal with the intrapsychic context within which these expressions of protest develop. Analysis of the culture's sex-role prescriptions, particularly for adolescents, helps clarify—at least after the fact—why they are among the particular targets of protest. Any act of protest should be interpreted in this dual way: for what it says about protesting individuals and those attracted to the dissident movement and also for what it may say about the social institutions against which the protest is aimed.

In discussing the conflicts faced by girls at adolescence, I have noted some that seem intimately related to the particular course of female sexual development at this stage; other conflicts, and even the outcome of some of the biologically induced conflicts, seem clearly to stem from a somewhat overspecial-

New sources of conflict in females at adolescence and early adulthood

ized, narrowly conceived set of sex-role expectations that is stringently imposed on adolescents in our culture.

References

Asayama, S. Comparison of sexual development of American and Japanese adolescents. *Psychologia*, 1957, **1,** 129–131.
Bardwick, J. *The psychology of women.* New York: Harper, 1970.
Benedek, T., & Rubenstein, B. B. Ovarian activity and psychodynamic processes. *Psychosomatic Medicine*, 1939, **1.**
Coleman, J. G. *The adolescent society.* New York: Free Press, 1961.
Deutsch, H. *Psychology of women.* New York: Grune and Stratton, 1945.
Douvan, E. Sex differences in adolescent character processes. *Merrill Palmer Quarterly*, 1960, **6,** 203–211.
Douvan, E., & Adelson, J. *The adolescent experience.* New York: Wiley, 1966.
Douvan, E., & Kaye, C. *Adolescent girls.* Ann Arbor: Survey Research Center, 1956.
Erikson, E. H. *Childhood and society.* New York: Norton, 1950.
Friedenberg, E. Z. *The vanishing adolescent.* Boston: Beacon, 1959.
Gold, M., & Williams, J. *The national survey of youth.* Ann Arbor: University of Michigan Press, 1969.
Horrocks, J. E., & Thompson, G. G. A study of friendship fluctuations of rural boys and girls. *Journal of Genetic Psychology*, 1946, **69,** 189–198.
Ivey, M. E., & Bardwick, J. M. Patterns of affective fluctuation in the menstrual cycle. *Psychosomatic Medicine*, 1968, **30** (3), 336–345.
Kagan, J. Acquisition and significance of sex typing and sex role identity. In M. L. Hoffman & L. W. Hoffman (Eds.), *Review of child development research*, Vol. I. New York: Russell Sage Foundation, 1964. Pp. 137–167.
Kagan, J., & Moss, H. A. *Birth to maturity.* New York: Wiley, 1962.
Kinsey, A. C., Pomeroy, W. B., Martin, C. E., et al. *Sexual behavior in the human male.* Philadelphia: Saunders, 1948.
Kinsey, A. C., Pomeroy, W. B., Martin, C. E., et al. *Sexual behavior in the human female.* Philadelphia: Saunders, 1953.
Mead, M. *Male and female.* New York: Morrow, 1949.
Murray, H. A., et al. *Thematic apperception test manual.* Cambridge, Mass.: Harvard University Press, 1943.
Mussen, P. H., & Boutourline-Young, H. Relationships between rate

of physical maturing and personality among boys of Italian descent. *Vita Humana,* 1964, **7,** 186–200.

Newcomb, T. *Personality and social change.* New York: Dryden, 1943.

Sanford, R. N., et al. Physique, personality and scholarship. *Monographs of the Society for Research in Child Development,* 1943, No. 1.

Sanford, N. (Ed.) Personality development through the college years. *Journal of Social Issues,* 1956, **12** (4).

Stone, C. P., & Barker, R. G. Aspects of personality and intelligence in postmenarcheal and premenarcheal girls of the same chronological ages. *Journal of Comparative Psychology,* 1937, **23,** 439–455.

Stone, C. P., & Barker, R. G. The attitudes and interests of premenarcheal and postmenarcheal girls. *Journal of Genetic Psychology,* 1939, **54,** 27–71.

Symonds, P. M. *Adolescent phantasy.* New York: Columbia University Press, 1949.

Tangri, S. Role-innovation in occupational choice among college women. Unpublished doctoral dissertation, University of Michigan, 1969.

Thompson, G. G., & Horrocks, J. E. A study of the friendship fluctuations of urban boys and girls. *Journal of Genetic Psychology,* 1947, **70,** 53–63.

Witkin, H. A., et al. *Personality through perception, an experimental and clinical study.* New York: Harper, 1954.

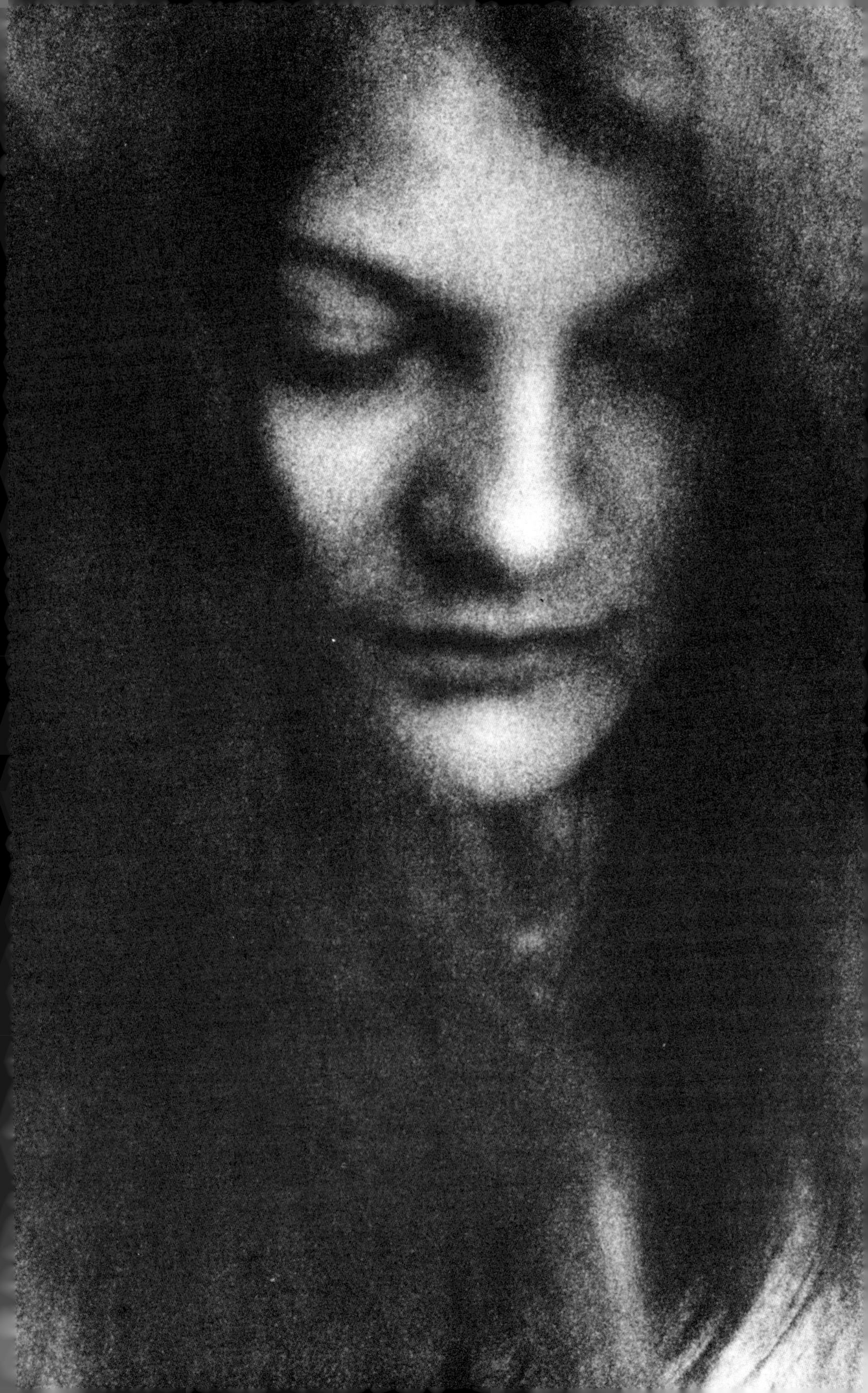

3

femininity and successful achievement: a basic inconsistency

Matina S. Horner

"Each step forward in work as a successful American regardless of sex means a step back as a woman...."

Margaret Mead
Male and Female

Although Mead first made this observation in 1949, it continues to be significant in today's society. Both in theory and in practice, the role of women in American society (which is primarily an achievement-oriented system) has over the years been little understood and much ignored by psychologists. A peculiar paradox arises in the society because we have an educational system that ostensibly encourages and prepares men and women identically for careers that social and, even more importantly, internal psychological pressures really limit to men. This paradox is reflected by the feelings of the women who somehow overcome these pressures and pursue a particular career: They feel anxious, guilty, unfeminine, and selfish.

Women as well as men in this society are immersed in a culture that rewards and values achievement and that stresses self-reliance, individual freedom, self-realization, and the full development of individual resources, including one's intellectual potential. In *The Achieving Society* (1961), McClelland has carefully elaborated how these values and attitudes (which are rooted in Max Weber's "Protestant Ethic") effect child-rearing practices that foster the development of achievement motivation. Winterbottom's (1958) work has shown that, when early self-reliance and mastery are expected and rewarded by the parents, the child internalizes these values and is prone to develop a high achievement motive (n Achievement). (This behavior will not occur, however, if the parents' high standards of excellence and independence reflect authoritarianism or rejection or simply the desire to make their own burdens less.)

Despite the prevalence of these values in most middle-class American homes, femininity and individual achievement continue to be viewed as two desirable but mutually exclusive ends. The cultural attitudes toward appropriate sex roles have truly limited the horizons of women. As a result, there is a significant and increasing absence of American women in the mainstream of thought and achievement in the society. For instance, the *proportion* of women college *graduates* is smaller today than it was 30 years ago, even though in absolute numbers more women are being educated. Furthermore, although the *number* of working women is increasing, the vast majority are found in low-skilled jobs and a very small proportion are working at a level close to that reflecting their educational or professional training. Whereas the number of professional women in Europe has doubled in the past 30 years, the number in America has actually declined. There are fewer women in upper-echelon positions now than there were before World War II. Thus a great number of women have been highly educated and trained for various professions or positions of leadership but are not using their skills, even though they may be part of the labor force at some lower level. This situation reflects the greatest loss of potential.

Although the social structure decries the terrible loss of female potential in both economic and personal terms, it provides few, if any, positive incentives or sanctions for career-oriented women. This situation is particularly noticeable for women of middle- or upper-class status who want to work for reasons other than economic necessity or survival. For women the distinction between a "job" and a "career" is very important.

Recently the "intellectual community" has been exerting effort to come to some understanding of the loss of human potential and resources that is reflected in this pattern of behavior. The experimental data to be presented later in the chapter show that, despite the removal for women of many legal and educational barriers to achievement, which existed until the 20th century, there remains a *psychological barrier* that is considerably more subtle, stubborn, and difficult to overcome. I refer to this barrier as the *motive to avoid success* (M_{-s}). This "fear of success" receives its impetus from the expectancy held by women that success in achievement situations will be followed by negative consequences, including social rejection and the sense of losing one's femininity.

It has been difficult to identify the nature of the psychological barrier to achievement in women. Therefore, before continuing, it would be useful to consider briefly the nature of the Expectancy-Value theory of motivation and the data that provided the background for developing this notion. In attempting to understand the motivational process, Expectancy-Value theory places equal emphasis on the significance of two elements. The first element is a stable, enduring personality characteristic called *motive* (M). The second element comprises two specific, immediate, but more transient, properties of the environment that define the challenge offered by the situation: the expectancy (E) or probability of a certain outcome occurring, and the incentive value (I) or attractiveness of that outcome to the person in question. Within the theory an important distinction is made between *motive* and *motivation*. Before any motive can influence behavior, it must become motivation; that is, the motive must be aroused by one's expectancy of the consequences of his actions and by the incentive value of the expected consequences. For example, in the Theory of Achievement Motivation (Atkinson & Feather, 1966) it is assumed that the strength of one's motivation to achieve success (T_s) is determined by a multiplicative interaction between the *strength of the motive to achieve success* (M_s); *the expectancy or probability of success* (P_s) in the specific situation, which is defined by the difficulty of the task; and *the incentive value of success* (I_s), which has been shown to be inversely related to task difficulty ($I_s = 1 - P_s$). Mathematically, then,

$$T_s = M_s \times P_s \times I_s.$$

It should be stressed that one's expectation of the consequences of his actions is an extremely important variable for determining the strength of his (achievement) motivation.

The particulars and mathematical derivations of the Theory of Achievement Motivation are presented only to clarify the distinction between motive and motivation; they need not concern us beyond that point. However, it *is* important to remember that positive motivation to do something is aroused by the expectancy that one's behavior will be followed by positive consequences. On the other hand, the expectancy or anticipation of negative consequences produces anxiety, which is a tendency to *inhibit* the activity. Once negative motivation or

Strength of
Motivation
to
Approach
Success
(T_S)

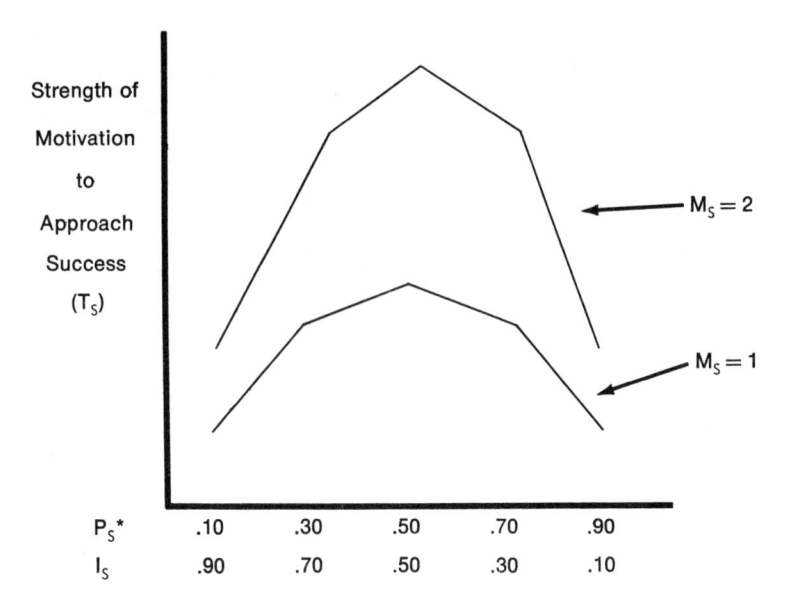

$M_S = 2$

$M_S = 1$

| P_S* | .10 | .30 | .50 | .70 | .90 |
| I_S | .90 | .70 | .50 | .30 | .10 |

*P_S = expectancy of success

Figure 1. Tendency to approach success = $T_S \times M_S \times P_S \times I_S \times (I_S = 1 - P_S)$

anxiety is aroused in a situation, it weakens the strength of all positive motivation for undertaking or persisting at the activity expected to have negative consequences.

Since the publication of *The Achievement Motive* (McClelland, Atkinson, Clark, & Lowell, 1953) extensive research has been directed toward understanding the contemporaneous determinants of achievement-oriented behavior. As a result, there is a very impressive and theoretically consistent body of data related to achievement motivation and its sources, development, assessment, and impact on the performance of men. This evidence shows the effects of individual differences in achievement motivation on the kinds of risks preferred and taken, the levels of aspiration set, and the levels of performance and persistence shown by men in various types of achievement-oriented activity. The early work shows that male subjects who are high in achievement motivation prefer and do best at tasks of intermediate rather than extreme levels of difficulty (Atkinson & Litwin, 1960), that they set intermediate, realistic levels of aspiration (Mahone, 1958), and that they select work partners of high ability (French, 1956). In general they perform

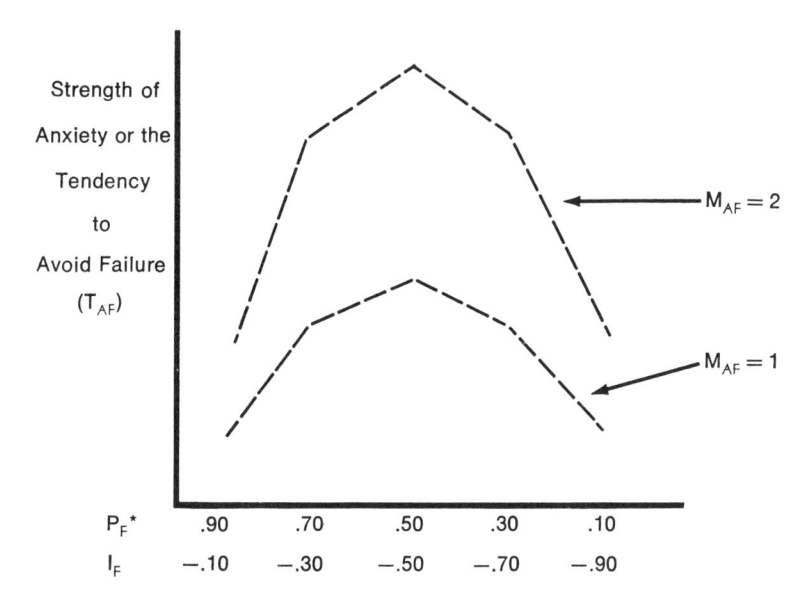

Strength of Anxiety or the Tendency to Avoid Failure (T_{AF})

| P_F* | .90 | .70 | .50 | .30 | .10 |
| I_F | −.10 | −.30 | −.50 | −.70 | −.90 |

*P_F = expectancy of failure

Figure 2. Tendency to avoid failure = $M_{AF} \times P_F \times I_F \times I_F = -P_S$

better and persist longer at all kinds of tasks in which some element of risk is involved (preferably 50–50), provided that the outcome depends on their ability rather than on chance and that the results will be made known and evaluated in terms of some standard of excellence (Atkinson, 1958).

Following these early results, the work in achievement motivation has gone mainly along two distinct lines.

McClelland has been primarily concerned with the social origins and molar social consequences of achievement motivation for society (McClelland, 1961). He has provided compelling evidence for his hypothesis that high achievement motivation is at least partly responsible for a high level of entrepreneurial activity, which in turn leads to the economic growth and development of a society. Particularly interesting and novel in their approach are the studies that relate the presence of achievement motivation to the economic growth and decline of certain societies in the past. This evidence is deduced from content analyses of samples of literature, such as folktales and children's readers, at critical points in these societies' histories. McClelland concludes that the risk-taking activities and

Femininity and successful achievement: a basic inconsistency

new ideas tried by entrepreneurs result from a strong motive to achieve and not merely from a strong "need for money," as is more generally suspected. More recently McClelland has been involved with research in motivation training as a tool for instituting behavioral change, particularly in underdeveloped or unmotivated sectors of society. This approach raises many interesting theoretical questions.

Atkinson and his coworkers (see Atkinson & Feather, 1966) have carried on a very systematic and impressive experimental analysis of the contemporaneous determinants of achievement-oriented activities. Their work has evolved from a continuous interaction between theoretical speculation and empirical data and is a very useful and stimulating guideline for further work in the area. As a result of this work, we now have a systematic theory and a large, consistent body of data about achievement motivation in men.

Data for females, on the other hand, have been scarce. Atkinson (1958) filled more than 800 pages with a compilation of available theory and data on achievement motivation. The question of sex differences was treated only in a footnote. It is admittedly a long footnote in which he refers to the issue of sex differences as "perhaps the most persistent unresolved problem in research on *n* Achievement" (p. 33). Even more striking is the absence of any mention of achievement motivation in women by McClelland (1961). Using evidence from vases, flags, doodles, and childen's books, he was able to study achievement motivation in such diverse samples as Indians, Quakers, and Ancient Greeks but not in women. This was not an oversight by either author; there are in fact not many meaningful data. The few results collected on female subjects have not been consistent with the existing theory of achievement motivation, with the findings for men, or even internally with one another. In other words, there has been neither a systematic theory nor a consistent body of data about achievement motivation in women. To add to the confusion, the sparse data that have been collected were gathered using very dissimilar methods and widely diverse samples of female subjects. As a result, it is nearly impossible to come to any meaningful conclusions.

We have not been able to explain women's inconsistent pattern of responses on the Thematic Apperception Test (TAT), which is used to assess individual differences in strength of the achievement motive, or to account for the lack of any consistent relationship between achievement motivation and performance in female subjects. Explanations offered in terms of a differential perception of what kind of striving behaviors are appropriate to their sex role have proven at best incomplete and premature.

It would be valuable now to consider briefly how achievement motivation is assessed and then to explore more carefully the nature of the sex differences that have been observed in studies of achievement motivation and behavior.

Beginning with the traditional clinical assumption that human motives are readily expressed in fantasy or imaginative behavior, and using the basic procedures developed by experimental psychologists for manipulating strength of motivation, McClelland et al. (1953) found, first with hunger and then with achievement, affiliation, and so on, that one could indeed validly and reliably assess individual differences in motive strength by analyzing fantasy or imaginative behavior. The particular criteria used for determining strength of achievement motivation were established by experimental fact, and a definitive scoring manual was developed (McClelland et al., 1953, Chap. 4; Atkinson, 1958, Chap. 12). Achievement imagery is reflected by concern with standards of excellence and with performing well, by unique accomplishments like inventions, by persistent and varying attempts to achieve, and by good or bad feelings about the consequences of the efforts. It is generally assumed that those who express the most achievement imagery under standard cues and testing procedures are the ones most highly motivated to achieve.

The major sex difference—at least the one that has received the greatest amount of attention—has been that women, unlike men, fail to show an increase in their achievement-imagery score when they are exposed to experimental conditions that arouse achievement motivation by stressing "intelligence and leadership ability" (Veroff, Wilcox, & Atkinson, 1953). Under neutral conditions the scores of women are as high or higher than those of men. McClelland points out that the two possible explanations considered, invalidity of the scoring system for women and scores too high to go higher, have been eliminated by experimental evidence. He concludes: "Apparently the usual arousal instructions simply do not increase achievement striving in women. . . ." Why is this type of arousal ineffective for women? The evidence from the more recent studies on women's motivation to avoid success provides a much clearer un-

Femininity and successful achievement: a basic inconsistency

derstanding of this problem. The earlier studies, which we shall consider only briefly, have given us a generally inconsistent pattern of results.

A study by Field (1951) suggests that achievement motivation in women can be aroused by referring to their social acceptability rather than to their "intelligence and leadership ability." On the other hand, Angelini's (1955) data on Brazilian university women argue that "intelligence and leadership" arousal *is* effective provided the sample used is made up of highly competitive women who value intellectual accomplishment. The implication is that women at large American coed universities (like that at which the previous work was done) are more socially than intellectually oriented. Lesser, Krawitz, and Packard (1963) tested Angelini's hypothesis within American society. They conducted their study at Hunter High School for girls in New York City. The school places great emphasis on the intellectual accomplishments of women. Admission is very competitive (only 150 of 4,000 highly selected candidates are admitted), and more than 99% of the graduates go on to college. A large percentage of these girls pursue professional careers. The results of the study were disappointing. Despite the fact that these girls are highly competitive and value intellectual accomplishments, no overall increase in achievement imagery was found under arousal conditions stressing intelligence and leadership ability. However, an interesting pattern of interaction was noted. The impact of the arousal condition on the TAT responses of the girls who were doing well at the school, compared with those who were not (with IQ scores matched), varied depending on whether the dominant stimulus figure on the TAT cue was male or female. The "achievers" showed an increase in achievement-motivation score under arousal conditions only to pictures of females and the "underachievers" only to pictures of males. Assuming that most of the girls who go to Hunter value achievement and see it as a relevant goal (or at least their parents do), the explanation offered for these results in terms of differential perception of social role among the girls is reasonable but not sufficient. For instance, why should the achievers—the girls who do well and presumably value achievement more than those who do not do well—show an increase in achievement motivation to female pictures, most of which depict women involved with traditional activities?

Other studies have attempted to relate such factors as individual value orientation, achievement relevance of goals, sex of the TAT stimulus figure, nature of arousal conditions (French & Lesser, 1964), and sex-role orientation (Lipinski, 1965) to achievement-motive scores and to performance. The results have been so inconsistent that, instead of resolving the problem of achievement motivation in women, they have only further emphasized the vast complexity of the issue.

The other major area of divergence between data for men and those for women has been the relationship between achievement motivation and performance. As already indicated, individual differences in strength of achievement motivation predict several types of performance for men in a theoretically consistent way but lack predictive power for women, for whom the results are both confusing and inconsistent. It is easy to see why most researchers in the area gave up on women and concentrated their efforts on the problems of achievement motivation and behavior in men. Freud (1965), in his attempts to understand women, began by pointing out that "throughout the ages the problem of women has puzzled people of every kind" (p. 154). Unsatisfied by his own efforts, he concluded that "if you want to know more about femininity, you must interrogate your own experience or turn to the poets, or else wait until science can give you more profound and more coherent information" (p. 185). But science, too, has had its problems in this area.

Some of the difficulties I have been discussing began to be clarified for me when I directed my attention beyond the achievement motive per se. Spurred on by data reporting a higher incidence of anxiety in women than in men, I became concerned with "achievement-related anxieties" that might be aroused along with the achievement motive in achievement-oriented situations.

In any achievement-oriented situation, performance is evaluated against some standard of excellence; thus the situation simultaneously offers both a chance for success and a threat of failure. The achievement motive is aroused by the expectancy that good performance will lead to a positive feeling like pride, the motive to avoid failure (test anxiety) is aroused by the expectancy that poor performance will lead to a negative feeling like shame. Measuring both types of motivation in men markedly enhances the predictive power of Atkinson's Theory of Achievement Motivation (Atkinson & Litwin, 1960; Atkinson & Feather, 1966).

Femininity and successful achievement: a basic inconsistency

Test or achievement anxiety has long been viewed primarily as motivation to avoid failure. Recently, however, I have entertained the hypothesis that women may in fact be more anxious than men in testing or achievement-oriented situations because they face negative consequences and hence anxiety not only in failing but also in succeeding. The anxiety-provoking aspects of success probably lie in the aggressive, masculine overtones that are implicit in or generally associated with successful competition in achievement situations. As I have already indicated, I refer to this disposition to become anxious in competitive achievement situations as the motive to avoid success. The anxiety is aroused whenever one expects that success will lead to negative consequences.

What exactly are the negative consequences of success in competitive achievement activity for women, and why has it taken us so long to recognize them? Perhaps part of our inability to recognize the problems results from a general lack of awareness of the extent to which we have been influenced by the image of woman and her sex role that has evolved over the centuries. Aristotle claimed that women never suffered from baldness because they never used the contents of their heads. That image of woman appears to have persisted over the centuries. Recall for a moment the misguided lamentations of the misogynic Professor Higgins in *My Fair Lady:*

> *Why Can't a Woman Be More Like a Man?*
> Women are irrational
> Their heads are full of cotton, hay, and rags.
> Why can't a woman learn to use her head?
> Why is thinking something women never do?

One wonders if this image might not be a more accurate reflection of our society's attitudes than we care to admit. While half-seriously attempting to answer Professor Higgins, we can perhaps pinpoint the source of anxiety about success: Let us consider what happens when women stray from the image and do use their heads.

If not rejected, they are praised (or castigated) for having Masculine Minds. Clare Booth Luce rejected that kind of praise from a colleague by saying: "I must refuse the compliment that I think like a man. Thought has no sex. One either thinks or one does not." Other women who are actively engaged in professional pursuits find themselves constantly trying to establish or prove their femininity, often going to great efforts and sometimes to extremes to display in dress and speech the obvious popular standards of femininity. Conrad suggested that "A woman with a masculine mind is not a being of superior efficiency; she is simply a phenomenon of imperfect differentiation—interestingly barren and without importance."

Unfortunately, many people unconsciously connect sex with certain characteristics and occupations. Although there is nothing intrinsically feminine about typing or teaching, or intrinsically masculine about medicine, physics, investment counseling, preaching, or just plain "thinking," for that matter, we have had difficulty adjusting to this idea psychologically. As a whole, society has been unable to reconcile personal ambition, accomplishment, and success with femininity. The more successful or independent a woman becomes, the more afraid society is that she has lost her femininity and therefore must be a failure as a wife and mother. She is viewed as a hostile and destructive force within the society. On the other hand, the more successful a man is in his work (as reflected in his high status, salary, and administrative powers—all of which are in keeping with his masculinity), the more attractive he becomes as a spouse and father. Whereas men are unsexed by failure (Mead, 1949), women seem to be unsexed by success.

Maccoby (1963) has pointed out that "the girl who maintains qualities of independence and active striving (achievement-orientation) necessary for intellectual mastery defies the conventions of sex appropriate behavior and must pay a price, *a price in anxiety.*" This observation may help explain why, after four years at a very high-ranking women's college (during which time they became "more liberal and independent"—that is, more masculine—in their values and attitudes), girls show a higher incidence of anxiety and psychological disturbance than they did when they were freshmen (Sanford, 1961, Chap. 24).

At a symposium on the potential of women in which Mannes (1963) discussed the problems of the creative woman and described the "entrance charges" she must pay for the approval of men and other women, the point was made that "nobody objects to a woman's being a good writer or sculptor or geneticist *if*, at the same time, she manages to be a good wife, a good mother, good-looking, good-tempered, well-dressed, well-groomed, and *unaggressive.*"

Most American women faced with the conflict between

Femininity and successful achievement: a basic inconsistency

maintaining their feminine image and developing their ability compromise by disguising that ability and abdicating from competition in the outside world. Consider little Sally (from the *Peanuts* comic strip), who remarked, "I never said I wanted to be someone. All I want to do when I grow up is be a good wife and mother. So—why should I have to go to kindergarten?" We are all familiar with the American coed who is intelligent enough to do well but also too intelligent to get all As and thereby lose her man. She knows she will be more "desirable" if she needs the assistance of a male Galahad to help her understand her work. Women have been choosing—perhaps unconsciously—not to develop either their potential or their individuality but rather to live through and for others. This behavior is consistent with Rousseau's idea that a woman's "dignity consists in being unknown to the world; her glory is in the esteem of her husband; her pleasures in the happiness of her family."

Thus, while society has been legally opening its doors to women and decrying the loss of female potential, it has been teaching them to fail outside the home. No one ever seriously objects to a woman's education or intellectual development, provided its objective is to make her a more entertaining companion and a more enlightened, and thus better, wife and mother. Only when her objective is an independent personal career does a problem arise. Mead suggested that intense intellectual striving (of the kind necessary for the serious pursuit of a career) is viewed as "competitively aggressive behavior." The aggressive overtones of competition and success are evident in the fact that each time one person succeeds, someone else fails or is beaten. This situation may well be the basis of fear of success. It seems there is nothing more distasteful than an "uppity" woman who opts to beat a man, especially at "his own game"—be it law, medicine, physics, or rational thought. She will evoke the wrath not only of men but also of other women. Riesman (1964) points out that "women, as with many minority groups, bitterly resent and envy those among them who break out of confinement" and are frequently "shrewish and vindictive toward them."

Freud (1965) pointed out that the whole essence of femininity lies in repressing aggressiveness. A woman is threatened by success because unusual excellence in academic and intellectual areas is unconsciously equated with loss of femininity; as a result, the possibility of social rejection becomes very real. A woman who achieves success may lose her self-esteem and her sense of femininity, which is an internalized standard acquired early in the socialization process. Thus, regardless of whether anyone else finds out about her success, the inconsistency between femininity and successful achievement is so deeply embedded that most women, as Rossi (1965) has indicated, believe that even wanting something more than motherhood is unnatural and reflects emotional disturbance within them. Social rejection following success can also prevent a woman from fulfilling her other needs for affection, love, marriage, and children. Kagan and Moss (1962) summarize the problem and its consequences as follows:

> The typical female has greater anxiety over aggressiveness and competitive behavior than the male. She therefore experiences greater conflict over intellectual competition which in turn leads to inhibition of intense strivings for academic excellence.

Assuming that, for most men, active striving for success in competitive achievement activity is consistent with masculinity and self-esteem and does not give rise to the expectancy of negative consequences, it may be that the motive to avoid success is one of the major factors underlying sex differences detected in research on achievement-related motivation and performance.

Under achievement-oriented conditions that stress "leadership or intellectual ability," women may inhibit expression of their achievement motivation on the TAT because of the concurrent arousal of anxiety about failure and anxiety about success. Thus women's TAT scores may not be an accurate or valid measure of the strength of their achievement motive and cannot be expected to relate to performance in the same way that men's scores do. It would be consistent within the Expectancy-Value framework to argue that it is precisely those women who are most able or most motivated to achieve whose scores will be most adversely affected by the motive to avoid success. Only if a woman desires or is capable of attaining success in a situation can she expect the negative consequences; without this expectation, anxiety or motivation to avoid success will not be aroused.

It is evident in psychoanalytic literature that, in order to understand behavior, both anxiety and the defensive reactions

Femininity and successful achievement: a basic inconsistency

against that anxiety should be considered. Under achievement arousal, women may defensively project or express their achievement motivation to TAT cues that depict women engaged in less threatening or more traditional types of activity or to pictures of men engaged in the more threatening, achievement-oriented types of activity. If less threatening cues are not available, expression of their achievement motive may be totally inhibited. These two options were available to the students in the Hunter High School study. The fact that, under arousal conditions, the "achievers" (presumably less anxious girls) showed an increase in achievement motivation to the female cues and the "underachievers" (presumably more anxious girls) to the male cues is consistent with the clinical assumption that projecting defensively to a same-sex figure engaged in less threatening activity reflects a lower level of anxiety than projecting to an opposite-sex figure engaged in the threatening activity.

I have noted that before any motive (any stable characteristic of one's personality) can influence behavior, it must become motivation; for example, it must be aroused by more specific, immediate, and transient characteristics of the environment (such as one's expectations about the consequences of his actions) and by the incentive values of the expected consequences. When the expectancies are negative, anxiety or negative inhibitory motivation results and interferes with performance. I have been suggesting that women can anticipate many negative consequences for actively seeking success in competitive achievement situations. A competitive situation is one in which performance reflecting intellectual and leadership ability is evaluated against a standard of excellence and also against the performance of one or more competitors.

Let us assume that anxiety about success—that is, anxiety about competitiveness and its masculine overtones—underlies many of the major sex differences detected in research on achievement motivation. It then follows that women should perform or behave differently in competitive and, by implication, aggressive achievement situations than in noncompetitive achievement situations. The negative incentive value of success should be greater for women if the success is attained under interpersonal competitive conditions, especially if the competitors are men and even more so if they are "important" men, such as mates or prospective boyfriends. It is in this last situation that the greatest weakening or inhibition of positive achievement motivation should occur.

Empirical Evidence

I will now present some of the empirical evidence in support of the ideas that have thus far been proposed and discussed. The first goal was to determine the extent of any sex differences in the motive to avoid success, and a measure to assess individual differences in this motive was developed (Horner, 1968). It involved a standard TAT for the achievement motive, except that four verbal, rather than pictorial, cues were used. An additional verbal lead was included that could be scored for motive to avoid success. For the 90 women in the study, the cue used was "After first-term finals, Anne finds herself at the top of her medical school class." The cue for the 88 men in the sample was "After first-term finals, John finds himself at the top of his medical school class." The subjects in this study were predominantly freshmen and sophomores at a large Midwestern coeducational university.

Precedents in the literature (Scott, 1958) show what happens in a TAT when a person is confronted with a cue or situation that represents a threat rather than a goal or that simultaneously represents a goal and a threat. These guidelines were used in developing the scoring criteria for "Fear of Success Imagery." Through a very simple present-absent system, the stories were scored for the motive to avoid success. "Fear of Success" was registered when the imagery expressed reflected serious concern about success, such as:

a. negative consequences *because of the success;*
b. anticipation of negative consequences *because of the success;*
c. negative affect *because of the success;*
d. instrumental activity away from present or future success, including leaving the field for more traditional female work such as nursing, schoolteaching, or social work;
e. any direct expression of conflict about success;
f. denial of *effort* in attaining the success (also cheating or any other attempt to deny responsibility or reject credit for the success);
g. denial of the situation described by the cue; or
h. bizarre, inappropriate, unrealistic, or nonadaptive responses to the situation described by the cue.

The subjects' responses can be readily classified into three main groups.

1. Fear of Social Rejection. This reaction appeared most frequently. The negative affect and consequences described were rooted mainly in affiliative concerns, including fear of being socially rejected and fear of losing one's friends or one's datability or marriageability. Fear of isolation or loneliness as a result of the success, as well as the desire to keep the success a secret and pretend that intelligence is not there, were also included. The following are examples of stories in this category.

Anne has a boyfriend, Carl, in the same class, and they are quite serious. Anne met Carl at college, and they started dating about their sophomore year in undergraduate school. Anne is rather upset and so is Carl. She wants him to be higher scholastically than she is. Anne will deliberately lower her academic standing the next term, while she does all she subtly can to help Carl. His grades come up and Anne soon drops out of med school. They marry and he goes on in school while she raises their family.

She is in a class of a great number of highly intelligent and competitive people, one of whom is her fiancé. . . . Anne is ambitious and has more innate ability than does her boyfriend. Anne is fearful that this situation will have a detrimental effect on their relationship and later on their marriage. Her superiority will mean that her eventual earning power will be greater. Although he would never let her know, her husband would resent that. It is important that Anne marry this man because of their closeness. But Anne will *never be entirely happy* in the marriage because she must always hold back her mentality and vocational desires.

Anne is a wonderful girl who has always succeeded. She never had to work. Anne didn't really care. She went to med school because she couldn't marry. . . . She really cares nothing and wants to get married. No one will marry her. She has lots of friends but no dates. She's just another girl. She tries to pretend intelligence is not part of her. She doesn't hide it—just ignores it. She will get a great job in a marvelous hospital. I don't know if she will ever marry.

Anne doesn't want to be number one in her class. She feels she shouldn't rank so high because of social reasons. She drops down to ninth in the class and then marries the boy who graduates number one.

2. Concern about One's Normality or Femininity. This group comprises stories in which negative affect and consequences are free of any affiliative concern and independent of whether anyone finds out about the success. Typical reactions in this category include doubting one's femininity, feeling guilt or despair about the success, and wondering about one's normality.

Anne has planned for a long time to be a doctor. She has worked hard in her schoolwork to enable her to learn better how to fulfill her dream. Now her hard work has paid off. Unfortunately, Anne suddenly no longer feels so certain that she really wants to be a doctor. She wonders if perhaps this isn't normal. . . . Anne decides not to continue with her medical work but to continue with courses that she never allowed herself to take before but that have a deeper personal meaning for her.

Anne is completely ecstatic but at the same time feels guilty. She wishes that she could stop studying so hard, but parental and personal pressures drive her. She will finally have a nervous breakdown and quit med school and marry a successful young doctor.

Anne cannot help but be pleased; yet she is unhappy. She had not wanted to be a doctor . . . she had half hoped her grades would be too poor to continue, but she had been too proud to allow that to happen. She had worked extraordinarily hard and her grades showed it. "It is not enough," Anne thinks. "I am not happy." She is not sure what she wants—only feels the pressure to achieve something, even if it's something she doesn't want. Anne says "To hell with the whole business" and goes into social work—not hardly as glamorous, prestigious, or lucrative; but she is happy.

The great amount of confusion manifested in this last story was not uncommon.

3. Denial. The stories in this third group were remarkable for their psychological ingenuity. Some of the girls denied the reality or possibility of the cue by actually changing its contents, distorting it, or simply refusing to believe it. Others tried to absolve Anne of responsibility for her success—as if it were some antisocial act. Also included in this group are the stories in which the success was attributed to cheating rather than to the girl's ability. Stories involving denial of various types made

Femininity and successful achievement: a basic inconsistency

up the second largest category and were particularly interesting.

Anne is a *code* name for a nonexistent person created by a group of med students. They take turns taking exams and writing papers for Anne. . . .

Anne is really happy she's on top, though Tom is higher than she—though that's as it should be. . . . Anne doesn't mind Tom winning.

Anne is talking to her counselor. The counselor says she will make a fine nurse. She will continue her med school courses. She will study very hard and find she can and will become a good nurse.

It was luck that Anne came out on top of her med class because she didn't want to go to med school anyway.

This last comment is an interesting reversal of the sour-grapes theme.

Several of the girls became very personally involved with Anne's dilemma: "I don't know. Her problem is apparently insoluble, because she is really a good student. Will she humble herself? Wait and see." or "I wonder if she will ever marry" or "The last I heard, she was still in school but had broken off her engagement." Others assumed the role of society and punished her for her accomplishment. The intensity, hostility, and symbolic quality of the language used by some of the girls was somewhat startling. They accused Anne of being a "social pariah"—someone who must "justify her existence." They attacked her physical attractiveness, her virtue, her sexuality, and sometimes even her person. For instance, in one story her classmates, "disgusted with her behavior . . . jump on her in a body and beat her. She is maimed for life." These stories in general tend to support Honoré de Balzac's contention that "A woman who is guided by the head and not the heart is a social pestilence: she has all the defects of a passionate and affectionate woman, with none of her compensations: she is without pity, without love, without virtue, without sex."

Overall, the two most common themes in the stories dealt with Anne's physical unattractiveness and with her "lonely Friday and Saturday nights." This result receives further support from some recent data gathered at an outstanding Eastern women's college. In an interview, the girls were told: "Anne is at the top of her med school class. Describe her." More than 70% of them described Anne as having an unattractive face, figure, or manners. Interestingly enough, more than 50% described her as "tall" (perhaps reducing the number of men who would find her attractive). The following are a few descriptions of Anne gathered from the interviews:

1. Snotty, conniving, goody-goody, conceited, brainy, tall.
2. Hard-working, devoted. Wears long skirts. Not feminine; tall, straight. Doesn't go out.
3. Masculine looking. Has short hair. Straight—doesn't smoke dope. Very smart, very competitive with men, not unattractive. Dates but not a steady boyfriend.
4. Quiet, until you get her going; meticulous—goes overboard in this way, not terribly concerned about her appearance. If she does go out, she probably goes out with older men or else she doesn't go out. Med students may be friends but only that. Not more intelligent than boys in her class but more willing to "grub" and do work. Driven person; maybe a liberal but not radical. Don't think she's examined whether it's all worthwhile.
5. Worked hard, but more than a machine. Really cool. Sincerely interested. Doesn't have to try hard. Bright, attractive, feminine. Surprises everyone.

This last description is an optimistic note from which to turn to the question of sex differences in the motive to avoid success. The sheer magnitude of the differences in the kind of responses made to the TAT cues by men and women in the first study was very striking. As had been hypothesized, the women did in fact show significantly more evidence of motive to avoid success than did the men. Only 8 out of 88, or less than 10%, of the men, compared with 59 out of 90, or more than 65%, of the

Table 1. *Sex differences in the motive to avoid success*

Motive to Avoid Success	Males	Females	χ^2	p
High	8	59	58.055	0.0005
Low	80	31		

women, wrote stories high in fear of success imagery. The percentage of white women showing fear of success imagery in response to this cue has been consistently between 62% and 75% in all the subsequent studies.

Perhaps the best way to understand the sex differences found is to consider a few of the typical stories written by men.

John is a conscientious young man who worked hard. He is pleased with himself. John has always wanted to go into medicine and is very dedicated. His hard work has paid off. He is thinking that he must not let up now, but must work even harder than he did before. His good marks have encouraged him (he may even consider going into research now). While others with good first-term marks sluff off, John continues working hard and eventually graduates at the top of his class.

The positive affect, increased striving, and heightened level of aspiration following success that are found in this and many of the other male stories are strikingly different from the typical female responses. The following story clarifies the positive impact that successful achievement has on the social relationships of men.

John is very pleased with himself, and he realizes that all his efforts have been rewarded: He has finally made the top of his class. John has worked hard, and his long hours of study have paid off. He spent hour after hour in preparation for finals. He is thinking of his girl, Cheri, whom he will marry at the end of med school. He realizes he can give her all the things she desires after he becomes established. He will go on in med school making good grades and be successful in the long run.

We have observed great differences in the presence of fear of success imagery in men and women based on differences in the expected consequences of successful achievement. It is reasonable therefore to speculate that the motive to avoid success is in fact a major variable underlying previously unresolved sex differences in studies of achievement motivation.

The next issue to consider is how—if at all—individual differences in the motive to avoid success affect behavior in achievement-oriented situations. Inasmuch as motives affect performance only when they are aroused, we should expect to see the behavioral manifestations of motivation to avoid success only in competitive achievement conditions in which success implies aggressiveness and behavior unbecoming to a "lady." Anxiety aroused by the expectancy of negative consequences of successful competition and by its aggressive overtones is assumed to be most prevalent in the most able or highly motivated women who are competing against men, particularly if they are doing so in male-dominated fields.

In the study designed to explore some of these hypotheses (Horner, 1968), each girl was administered a number of tasks in a large mixed-sex competitive condition (not unlike a large classroom or lecture situation). The girls were then randomly assigned to three other experimental conditions. Some were placed in a strictly noncompetitive (NC) situation in which they worked on a number of tasks guided only by tape-recorded instructions. The rest of the girls were divided at random between two competitive situations in which they worked on the same tasks and followed the same instructions as did those girls in the NC situation. In one of these two groups each girl competed against one male and in the other group against one female. None of the girls knew or had previous contact with the competitors. Performance in the initial large group condition was most highly related to that in the two-person, opposite-sex competitive condition. This result is reasonable, since the large group also involved members of both sexes. Only the 30 subjects in the NC condition worked in both a competitive and a noncompetitive situation.

It was important to exert some control over initial ability differences between the subjects; otherwise, I could not have determined how much of the difference in performance stemmed from motivation and how much from initial ability differences. In this study the best control possible was letting each subject act as her own control—that is, perform in both the competitive and noncompetitive setting. Thus the performance of the 30 women in the NC situation was compared with their own previous performance in the large mixed-sex situation. The tasks involved were two standard, similar, and highly correlated verbal tasks.

The results from this part of the study are shown in Table 2. Clearly, the women who score high in fear of success imagery do better working alone than they do in the competitive condition, whereas those who score low in fear of success imagery

Femininity and successful achievement: a basic inconsistency

Table 2. *The motive to avoid success and performance in competitive and noncompetitive achievement situations*

Motive to Avoid Success	Performed Better in Noncompetitive Situation	Performed Better in Competitive Situation
High	13	4
Low	1	12
	$\chi^2 = 11.374$	$p < 0.005$

do better in the competitive condition. The performance of this latter group of women resembles that of the men, who are generally low in fear of success imagery and two-thirds of whom do better in the competitive than in the noncompetitive situation.

On a questionnaire following performance, the high-fear-of-success women who worked in the competitive situations reported that it was significantly less important for them to do well on their tasks than it was for the women working alone in the noncompetitive condition. In other words, high-fear-of-success women working alone consider it more important to do well and probably try harder than do high-fear-of-success women working against a competitor. There are no differences in reported level of importance between the conditions for women low in fear of success imagery. Overall, subjects with high fear of success imagery report a lower level of importance for doing well than do those with low fear of success imagery.

Table 3. *Mean level of "importance" reported by women in response to the question "How important was it for you to do well on tests in this part of the experiment?" as a function of individual differences in fear of success imagery and experimental condition*

Fear of Success Imagery	Noncompetitive Condition NC			Competitive Condition Mixed Sex FM			Same Sex FF		
	N	M	σ	N	M	σ	N	M	σ
High	(17)	55.6	9.2	(19)	45.7	19.4	(20)	44.7	24.4
Low	(13)	66.5	24.0	(11)	61.1	27.1	(10)	56.5	12.3
	$t = 1.56; p < .10$			$t = 1.66; p < .05$			$t = 1.75; p < .05$		

For subjects with:
High Fear of Success Imagery   NC vs. FM $t = 1.99$ $p < .05$
                               NC vs. FF $t = 1.85$ $p < .05$
Low Fear of Success Imagery   No Significant Differences

The responses on the questionnaire are consistent with the performance data in suggesting that women—especially those high in motive to avoid success—will not fully explore their intellectual potential when they are in a competitive setting, especially when they are competing against men. Optimal performance for most women high in fear of success can be obtained only if they work in achievement settings that are noncompetitive. In the absence of interpersonal competition and its aggressive overtones, whereby the tendency to avoid success (T_{-s}) is minimally, if at all, aroused, these women will perform efficiently.

This study, as an exciting first step toward understanding the behavior of women in achievement situations, has raised many interesting and challenging questions. However, further explorations are needed. For instance, we will have to probe into the nature of both the personal and the situational factors that arouse motivation to avoid success as well as those that minimize its influence on performance. Particularly important and interesting will be studies on the developmental issues involved with respect to the motive to avoid success.

Some recent data (that are still being analyzed) show a very marked and progressive increase—both quantitative and qualitative—in fear of success imagery in two groups of girls: one from junior high to senior high and the other from the freshman to senior years in college. The increment is reflected in the increasing percentage of girls expressing fear of success imagery as well as in the increasing mean score of motive to avoid success in each group. The motive-to-avoid-success score for the girls in this study was based on responses to two cues, one of which was highly competitive and threatening and the other less so. The threatening cue involved successful competition against men in a male-dominated field like medicine or law. The second cue involved success in what we believed to be a less directly competitive, less masculine area such as the writing of a novel in one's spare time. The older girls responded with more fear of success imagery than did the younger group to the less threatening cue.

It is easy to conjecture why a senior, particularly in the college group, would show higher motivation to avoid success. As Sanford (1961) has indicated, the senior year in college is critical, especially for those girls who have not as yet become engaged. Most of the girls are convinced that it is more important to *be* a woman than to *become* some kind of specialist. It

Femininity and successful achievement: a basic inconsistency

is very clear to them that the brighter they are, and the more fully they extend and fulfill their potential, the more they restrict their choices or possibilities for marriage. Riesman (1964, pp. 731–732) has made the following observation on the subject:

> Just as girls six feet tall complain of the still taller men who marry girls who are five feet two, since there are not enough really tall men to go around, so girls who are six feet tall in intellect and drive realize that many men of comparable power will marry very low-pressure, eye-fluttering girls, and that there will not be enough secure, nondependent men left for the women who could grow and develop in marriage to such men. Hence girls who feel that if they do not marry early . . . they may not marry at all are prepared unconsciously if not consciously to surrender chances for personal distinction in order to be fairly sure of pleasing a larger range of men.

Thus for the girl who is a senior in college the conflict of marriage vs. career becomes very intense. The decision to pursue a higher level of education or a career as opposed to marriage and/or a job is usually made then and requires some degree of commitment. After all, a woman does not usually get a Ph.D. in biology, physics, or some other field to be a more entertaining companion or a more enlightened wife and mother. (These reasons are frequently given to "justify" college education for women.)

An important question that must now be considered is at what point and *why* motivation to avoid success becomes a significant factor in achievement-related behavior in women. What exactly are the major determinants of its arousal in the "real world"? In the early school years girls outperform boys, but at about the time of puberty—and perhaps coincidental with dating interests—the advantage is significantly reversed, particularly in nonverbal areas such as mathematics and science, which are traditionally viewed as "masculine." Interestingly enough, girls who are either engaged or married to "brilliant, successful, secure young men" have little difficulty maintaining their standing. No problem arises for them as long as he is viewed as the "smarter" or "more intelligent" of the two and the one against whom "competition would be hopeless."

There is increasing evidence that, in the course of their

college experience, most capable young women change their plans toward a less ambitious, more traditionally feminine direction—that is, away from "role innovation" (Tangri, 1969; Schwenn, 1970). We can now only speculate as to how much of this trend can be attributed to the arousal of the motive to avoid success and the fear of social rejection as a result of success. We must come to some understanding of what it is in the college experience that influences otherwise achievement-oriented, capable girls to change their plans. Komarovsky (1959) reports evidence of a sudden shift or reversal of parental pressures and approval for academic success. Whereas parents (and society) encourage girls to go to college and reward their good performance up to that point, they suddenly begin to evaluate their daughters "in terms of some abstract standard of femininity with an emphasis on marriage as the appropriate goal for girls of this age."

How important are these pressures, and are they reinforced by the girls' peers, both male and female? A long-term study would be valuable, especially if it followed young girls through adolescence, college, marriage, and career choice (if any). It should consider how both the development and expression of motivation to avoid success are influenced by parental and peer attitudes (as well as attitudes of "significant men" in the girls' lives) toward the role of women in contemporary life. A pilot study at an Eastern college on highly motivated or intelligent girls (the grades were all above $B-$) showed that the major role in the *arousal* of the motive to avoid success is played by the girls' male peers (Schwenn, 1970). A very interesting and suggestive pattern emerges from this study. The girls who showed evidence of motivation to avoid success or of anxiety about social rejection were those who either did not date at all (all had A averages) or who dated men who disapproved of "career women." They manifested their anxieties by refusing to divulge that they were doing well or had received an A (preferring to make their failures known) and by changing their future plans toward a more traditional, less ambitious career (or none at all) or even by deciding to drop out of school altogether. When asked how the boys in their lives responded to their aspirations—even the less ambitious ones— the girls frequently answered, "They laugh." Other replies included, "He thinks it's ridiculous for me to go to graduate school or law school. He says I can be happy as a housewife and I just need to get a liberal arts education" or "He wants a

Femininity and successful achievement: a basic inconsistency

wife who will be a mother full-time until the kids are grown" or "I am turning more and more to the traditional role because of the attitudes of my boyfriend and his roommates. I am concerned about what they think." This result is consistent with the finding that women are dependent on others for their self-esteem. Independence itself is inconsistent with the female image.

On the other hand, the girls who were not fearful of making their success known and who continued to strive for innovative careers were engaged to or seriously dating men who were not threatened by the girls' success. In fact, those men actively encouraged and expected the girls to do well. The girls indicated the support they received in such statements as:

"He wants me to be intelligent. It is a source of pride to him that I do so well."

"I would have to explain myself if I got a C. I want him to think I'm as bright as he is."

"He thinks it would be a good idea for me to go to law school."

"He feels very strongly that I should go to graduate school to get a master's degree. He does not want to feel that he has denied me a complete education."

One of the factors distinguishing the couples in the second group from those in the first is a mutual understanding that the boy is the more intelligent of the two. In the first group a tension is rooted between them in the fear that she is the more intelligent one. Other important factors stem from how threatening the boyfriend considers her present and future success: If they are in the same school, or taking the same courses, or planning to go to the same graduate school or have the same career, he will very likely feel threatened and resentful. Clearly the problems of achievement motivation in women involve more than a traditional view of the female role.

It would not be unreasonable at this point for us to speculate that what we have observed in the laboratory does in fact extend into and influence the intellectual and professional lives of women in our society. The arousal of motivation to avoid success may very well account for a major part of the withdrawal of so many trained American women from the mainstream of thought and achievement. We have already noted the great loss in human and economic resources that this withdrawal reflects.

The evidence presented here raises many questions about our educational system. For instance, is attendance at a same-sex educational institution more effective than attendance at a coed institution in reducing the impact of the motive to avoid success in girls? In the absence of competition against men, can the women develop their interests and explore their intellectual potential more fully? Many persons believe that they can. Recently Wellesley considered admitting men to the school, but several coeds protested, saying:

> How can a girl maintain her role as a woman when she is in intense academic competition with men, especially if she is excelling? Many capable girls have faced the frustration of accusations of aggressiveness, lack of femininity, and a desire to "beat the boys" when they were in high school and college . . . (*Harvard Crimson*, 1969).

The next question is whether the influence and support received at a same-sex institution continue after the women leave its protective atmosphere and again enter the "real world" of mixed-sex competition. The issue of competition being unfeminine is not especially relevant at an all-girls school. On the other hand, these girls do not have the opportunity presented to those at coeducational institutions to confront the problem and find ways to resolve it. These issues are presented rather clearly in comments made by two of the girls in the Radcliffe sample.

A girl who had attended an all-girls high school remarked:

> It had never entered my mind before I got here that I would be competing with boys. . . . You see the aggressive girls when you get here and you know it's the last thing in the world you want to be.

The other girl, who had attended a coed high school, observed:

> I used to feel self-conscious about being smart and getting good grades, but by my junior year in high school I had gotten over that . . . because I was a student leader and a cheerleader, too.

Femininity and successful achievement: a basic inconsistency

This last comment suggests that one way in which women who are successful in competitive achievement activities can resolve their anxiety about being unfeminine is to be equally successful in feminine tasks appropriate to their ages: cheerleading and dating in high school and later sexual attractiveness, cooking, motherhood, and so on.

It is clear that a psychological barrier exists in otherwise achievement-motivated and able women that prevents them from exercising their rights and fulfilling their potential. Even when legal and educational barriers to achievement are removed, the motive to avoid success will continue to inhibit women from doing "too well"—thereby risking the possibility of being socially rejected as "unfeminine" or "castrating." Unless we can find ways to prevent the motive from being aroused, our society will continue to suffer a great loss in both human and economic resources.

The negative feelings and consequences of a girl beating a boy in intellectual competition are poetically summarized by Whittier in his poem "In School Days." Having outperformed the boy in a spelling match, the girl says:

> "I'm sorry that I spelt the word:
> I hate to go above you,
> Because," —the brown eyes lower fell—
> "Because, you see, I love you."

At the end, despite her regrets, she too is "socially" rejected:

> Dear girl! The grasses on her grave
> Have forty years been growing!

References

Angelini, A. L. Un novo método para avaliar a motivação humano ("A new method of evaluating human motivation"). Unpublished doctoral dissertation, Universidade de São Paulo, Brazil, 1955. (Results summarized in Atkinson, 1958.)

Atkinson, J. W. (Ed.) *Motives in fantasy, action, and society.* Princeton, N. J.: Van Nostrand, 1958.

Atkinson, J. W., & Feather, N. T. *A theory of achievement motivation.* New York: Wiley, 1966.

Atkinson, J. W., & Litwin, G. H. Achievement motive and test anxiety conceived as motive to approach success and motive to avoid failure. *Journal of Abnormal and Social Psychology,* 1960, **60,** 52–63.

Field, W. F. The effects of thematic apperception on certain experimentally aroused needs. Unpublished doctoral dissertation, University of Maryland, 1951.

French, E. G. Motivation as a variable in work partner selection. *Journal of Abnormal and Social Psychology,* 1956, **53,** 96–99.

French, E. G. The interaction of achievement motivation and ability in problem solving success. *Journal of Abnormal and Social Psychology,* 1958, **57,** 306–309.

French, E. G., & Lesser, G. S. Some characteristics of the achievement motive in women. *Journal of Abnormal and Social Psychology,* 1964, **68,** 119–128.

Freud, S. *New introductory lectures on psychoanalysis.* New York: Norton, 1965. Lecture XXXIII.

Harvard Crimson, The. "Must Wellesley go coed to survive?" Dec. 16, 1969, p. 3.

Horner, M. Sex differences in achievement motivation and performance in competitive and noncompetitive situations. Unpublished doctoral dissertation, University of Michigan, 1968.

Kagan, J., & Moss, H. A. *Birth to maturity.* New York: Wiley, 1962.

Komarovsky, M. Functional analysis of sex roles. *American Sociological Review,* 1959, **15,** 508–516.

Lesser, G. S., Krawitz, R., & Packard, R. Experimental arousal of achievement motivation in adolescent girls. *Journal of Abnormal and Social Psychology,* 1963, **66,** 59–66.

Lipinski, B. G. Sex-role conflict and achievement motivation in college women. Unpublished doctoral dissertation, University of Cincinnati, 1965.

Maccoby, E. E. Woman's intellect. In S. M. Farber & R. H. L. Wilson (Eds.), *The potential of woman.* New York: McGraw-Hill, 1963. Pp. 24–39.

Mannes, M. The problems of creative women. In S. M. Farber & R. H. L. Wilson (Eds.), *The potential of woman.* New York: McGraw-Hill, 1963. Pp. 116–130.

Mahone, C. Fear of failure and unrealistic vocational aspiration. Unpublished doctoral dissertation, University of Michigan, 1958.

McClelland, D. C., Atkinson, J. W., Clark, R. A., & Lowell, E. L. *The achievement motive.* New York: Appleton, 1953.

McClelland, D. C. *The achieving society.* Princeton, N. J.: Van Nostrand, 1961.

Mead, M. *Male and female.* New York: Morrow, 1949. Also New York: Dell (Laurel Ed.), 1968.

Riesman, D. Two generations. *Daedalus*, 1964, **93**, 711–735.

Rossi, A. The case against full-time motherhood. *Redbook Magazine*, March 1965.

Sanford, N. (Ed.) *The American college.* New York: Wiley, 1961.

Schwenn, M. Arousal of the motive to avoid success. Unpublished junior honors paper, Harvard University, 1970.

Scott, W. A. The avoidance of threatening material in imaginative behavior. In J. W. Atkinson (Ed.), *Motives in fantasy, action, and society.* Princeton, N. J.: Van Nostrand, 1958. Chap. 40.

Tangri, S. Role-innovation in occupational choice. Unpublished doctoral dissertation, University of Michigan, 1969.

Veroff, J., Wilcox, S., & Atkinson, J. The achievement motive in high school and college-age women. *Journal of Abnormal and Social Psychology*, 1953, **48**, 103–119.

Winterbottom, M. R. The relation of need for achievement to learning experiences in independence and mastery. In J. W. Atkinson (Ed.), *Motives in fantasy, action, and society.* Princeton, N. J.: Van Nostrand, 1958. Chap. 33.

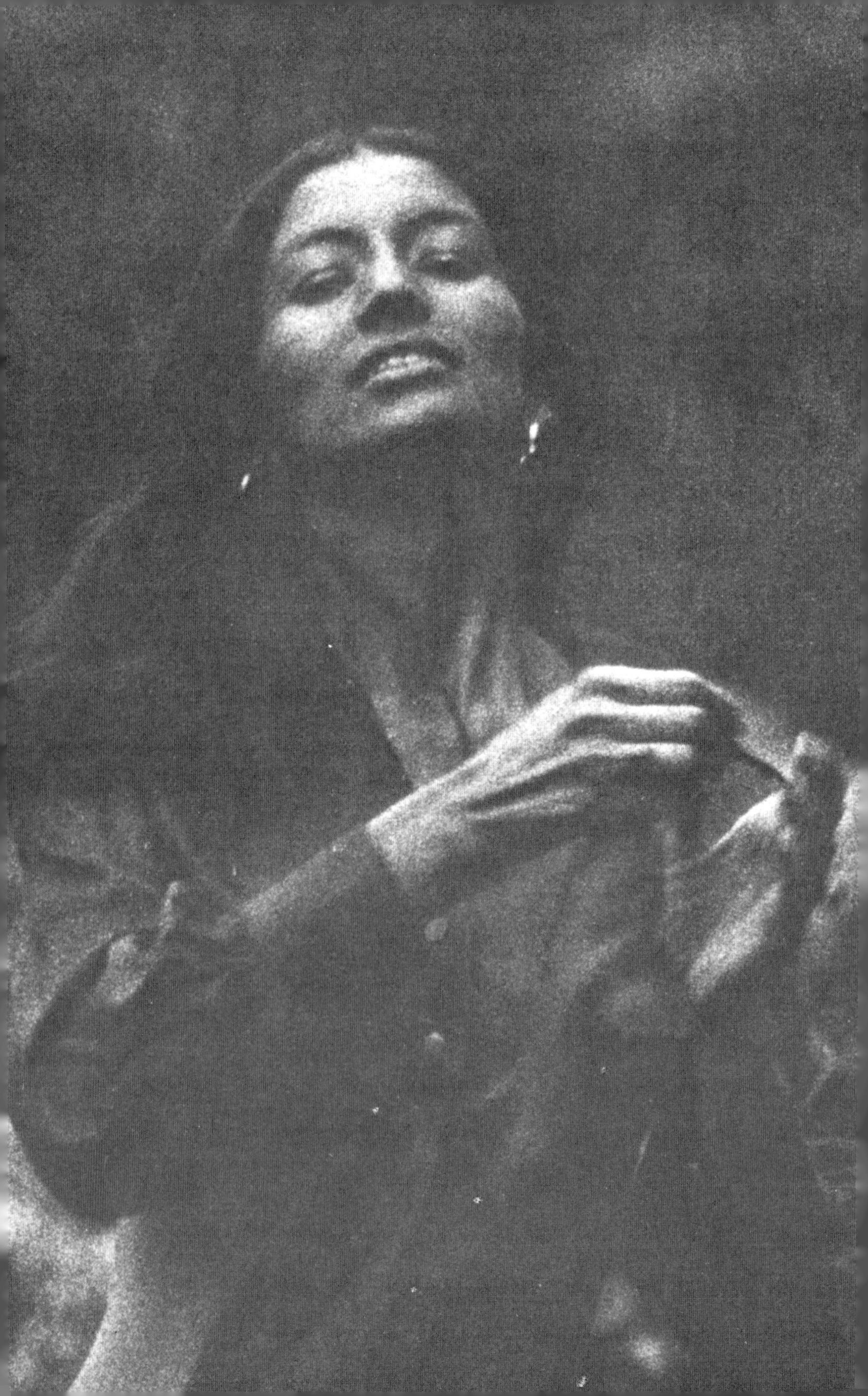

4

female ego styles and generational conflict

David Gutmann

Although the ideas I advance in this chapter are determinedly speculative, they have helped me order some personal observations made in this and other societies and have suggested some hypotheses for future empirical research. My main intent is to describe those ego styles—that is, those ways of creating and of managing experience—that discriminate between the sexes in predictable ways. I distinguish between the *autocentric* ego style, in which the order of events is seen as related to the self, and the *allocentric* ego style, in which the order of events is seen as having a direction and logic of its own.[1] The autocentric ego state, which is believed to characterize women, will receive major attention. I contend that it reflects nurture more than nature. Relevant to the United States and other, less "advanced," societies, I will present examples of masculine autocentricity, which has emerged as a dominant orientation among alienated youth. I believe that the alienation of young men results from the conflict between their autocentric ego style—which is based on ego diffusion, or lack of boundaries—and social institutions that both sponsor and require clear intrapersonal and interpersonal boundaries.

[1] The terms *allocentric* and *autocentric* were introduced by Schachtel (1959). For him these terms refer to distinct modes of relating to objects: the autocentric mode is a self-serving use of the object, and the allocentric mode recognizes the properties and needs of the object. As used in this chapter, these terms refer to the personal implications of social organization. That is, the autocentric social organization gives each individual recurrent experiences of being a focus or center of communal events and ties; the allocentric order conveys to the individual that the centers and sources of organization, social bonds, and initiatives are extraneous to him or that his alignment with such centers is not final and secure.

Ego Boundaries and Autocentricity in American Women

Throughout history, and in every culture, observers (usually male) have noted a tendency by females to leap to conclusions, to decide issues on emotional rather than rational grounds, and to ignore what men regard as the ruling necessities of existence. Freud (1925) rather peevishly explained that women have less reason than men to resolve the Oedipal conflict and thus fail to develop as stringent a superego:

I cannot escape the notion (though I hate to give it expression) that for women the level of what is ethically normal is different from what it is in men. Their superego is never so inexorable, so impersonal, so independent of its emotional origins as we require it to be in men. Character traits which critics of each epoch have brought against women—that they show less sense of justice than men, that they are less ready to submit to the great necessities of life, that they are often influenced in their judgment by feelings of affection or hostility—all these would be amply accounted for by the modification in the formation of their superego which we have already inferred.

A comparison of the responses of normal American males and females to the same set of Thematic Apperception Test (TAT) cards leads me to agree with Freud's description, if not with his "id-centered" explanation, of the "female" approach to the world. For example—as Freud might have predicted—I found that women are indeed more unpredictable and personalizing than men in their handling of the relatively ambiguous TAT stimuli. Men tend to approach the cards as a kind of puzzle or an exercise of the imagination. By and large, they realize that their stories, however reasonable, are at best possible interpretations and reflect their own imagination as much as the features of the stimulus. Thus, implicitly at least, men tend to take personal responsibility for their imaginings, which are recognized as such. But women tend not to maintain such a rational perspective or such distance and instead respond to the cards as if they actually *are* vivid or troubling events, rather than *possible* representations of them. For example, women may be disturbed by situations that they first read into the cards and then experience as a real event, separate from themselves and "out there." Thus women finish their stories with "I hope things turn out well for them" or "A boy like that should get what he deserves!"

The female subjects I studied were in effect saying that they had no responsibility for the situation they had constructed. For them their subjective fantasy had acquired, through the medium of the TAT card, a kind of objective reality over which they had, as they saw it, no control. One middle-aged woman was shown a specially prepared TAT card depicting an older man, an older woman, a younger man, and a younger woman engaged in some possibly domestic interaction. Whereas the typical story concerns contact between an older couple and a younger couple, this subject drastically shifted the partners: "The young man is married to the older woman, and the young woman is married to the older man. *And it shouldn't be that way!*" This subject had encountered her own sexual and possibly incestuous fantasy in the form of a "real" situation that she could then disavow.

In contrast to the male approach, the female approach lacks those qualities that are presumably fundamental to the secondary processes of the ego and, by extension, to successful adaptation: delay, objectivity, and especially *boundary*. That is, for women the boundary between self and other, or between the object and the emotion pertinent to that object, seems more tenuous or more permeable than is true for men. The world of women, as they map it onto the TAT, tends to be a metaphor—an extension of the affective reaction aroused in them by stimulating agents and events in their relevant domain. Thus, for women, stimulus, appraisal, and reaction are bonded together as parts of a continuous experience.

From the standpoint of an ego psychology that is perhaps biased toward masculine forms of adaptation, this "female" ego style would be stigmatized as regressive and even pathological. Accordingly, I was surprised to find that women seem to thrive within this rather boundaryless mode. By contrast, men who demonstrate a similarly diffuse approach to the TAT show up as neurotic on life-satisfaction and morale measures. But "unboundaried" women achieve higher scores on those scales than do the more contained and "boundaried" women. That is, those atypical women whose high boundaries match those of the normal male are more likely than either the typical boundaried man or the unboundaried woman to be anxious, depressed, or neurotic.[2]

Female ego styles and generational conflict

[2] These findings are discussed in greater detail in Gutmann (1964).

Ego Boundaries in the Autocentric Society

I was puzzled by this finding: Why should diffuse ego boundaries—often a precondition for male pathology—correlate positively with female zest and morale? I was further puzzled by the incidental results of subsequent cross-cultural studies carried out among various preliterate Mexican and American Indian groups: My TAT data indicated a similarity between the typical male Indian approach (regardless of tribe or region) and the *autocentric* approach of American women.

In these Indian societies the male-female differences first observed in the U.S. sample still emerged. Male Navajo or Maya ego functioning was more boundaried and objectifying than that of female Navajo or Maya. Yet, when American women and Indian males were compared against the same criteria for adequate ego functioning, they appeared to be similar, especially in regard to the construction and maintenance of ego boundaries. Thus, as with urban American *women*, I found among Maya and Navajo *men* the same tendencies to personalize the world, to confuse an imaginative construction with the stimulus that prompted that construction, and to confound what came from the self with what pertained to the stimulus. Like the better-adjusted American women, many culturally normal, reasonably contented, and competent Indian men lacked clear ego boundaries.[3]

Paradoxically, the male Indian examples eventually helped me to understand both the prevalence and the adaptive consequences of diffuse boundaries for American women. At the Indian sites I began to see an equivalence between social process and ego process that prompted the generalization that the Indian psychosocial ecology and the Indian ego were extensions of each other. The Indian ego seemed to be an internal continuation—a restatement in subjective terms—of a world that had organized its ways of receiving and creating experience. Now I could better understand that the low-boundary aspect of American women's ego functioning might be the result of a similar *adaptive* fit between the female ego and its special psychoecological circumstances. The following description of those aspects of the Indian psychosocial ecology that

[3] These findings, as well as the naturalistic interviewing method that provided the relevant data, are presented and discussed at greater length in Gutmann (1967).

bear on ego development will perhaps clarify the more general point in regard to American women.

In many ways the rather permeable Indian egos are reflections of the settings in which they develop. Comparing the general Indian environment with ours, I *experienced*, quite concretely, the degree to which our own postliterate, urban world balkanizes experience; by contrast, and despite the many differences between them, these Indian worlds are transitive—that is, they interrelate all culturally recognized agents in a kind of seamless unity. At even the most banal level one finds interpenetration of the extramural, "natural" order and the interior, "domestic" order: dwellings are formed outcroppings of their surrounding stone, clay, and thatch; pigs, chickens, and goats move in and out in their search for scraps. Socially, Indians *define* themselves and *know* themselves by clan and tribe names shared with those others who are, both conventionally and privately, much like themselves. Experience is redundant: what a person does today is a reasonable forecast of what he will do tomorrow; he has done, is doing, or will someday do largely what others have already done.

Linguistic usages in these societies tend to reflect and reinforce this sense of a coherent and redundant world. Especially among the Navajo, objects are defined in terms of the conventional actions that they elicit or imply: "Two Days' Canyon" is so named because of the time it takes the Navajo to journey through it. By the same token, actions cannot be considered or named apart from the particular agents toward which they are directed. For example, Navajo verbs are modified not only by person and tense but also by the object involved in the action that the verb implies. Objects and actions are blended into a continuous world, wherein there is relatively little separation of the personal from the social, of the objective from the subjective, of the abstract from the concrete.

Causation in these preliterate societies is understood not as a matter of process but of implication. Thus evil thoughts in the mind of one man can cause illness or misfortune to another man without an intervening agency: the evil intention *includes* the goal and thereby achieves it. Likewise, religious and medicine ceremonials tend to be stylized pictures of the state of affairs they are intended to bring about.

Clearly, in these Indian settings one could not normally develop a clear sense of where he ends and where others begin. On the contrary, these autocentric environments provide indi-

Female ego styles and generational conflict

viduals with recurrent experiences of continuity with or inclusion in those agents that have been made relevant to the self, either by cultural prescription or by personal experience. The sense of self is dispersed into, or includes, all those objects and agents that persistently provoke actions and affects from the ego. Indeed, in the autocentric world firm ego boundaries, as we know and value them in urban, *allocentric* society, can even be maladaptive—a sign and source of pathology.[4]

Ego Boundaries in the Allocentric Society

By contrast, allocentric environments are *impersonal*—that is, they do not take their order from the individual. They are unpredictable and subject to the whims of nature, the "laws of the market," or the inscrutable plans of remote leaders. These milieux pool together individuals and agents who are by and large intent on their own purposes—who will only recognize the existence of others if they interfere with or are necessary to the accomplishment of individual goals. On the personal level, allocentric domains provoke a chronic sense of self-other, subjective-objective boundaries, of discontinuity between fantasy and actuality, and of discontinuity between personal motives and the conventional guidelines of behavior. For the ego that matures within allocentric settings, the parts of the self are experienced as such—that is, as distinct from the external agents that are emotionally pertinent to them. Allocentricity is generally characteristic of men but also of literate and, especially, bourgeois urbanites, regardless of sex.

The Domestic Realm: An Autocentric Habitat

In psychoanalytic thinking, ego development is mainly a function of transactions on the ego-id interface. Diffuse ego

---

[4] For example, indigenous entrepreneurs are very often "premature" individualists who see their fate as separate from that of their fellow tribesmen, clansmen, or villagers. They typically enact their individuality by disregarding or breaching the conventions, and they thereby acquire a reputation for deviancy and witchcraft, especially if their "business" efforts meet with success. If they amass land and herds, their wealth is taken as proof of successful witchcraft. Thus, although the preliterate entrepreneur may operate out of a boundaried perspective, his neighbors take a more autocentric, personal view of his activity and its consequences and see in them evil rather than industry.

boundaries are attributed to early deficits in object relationships, hysteroid regression, or faulty superego development. In this chapter I have discussed the Indian environment at some length in order to support an alternative contention: that ego-society transactions can also influence the final form of ego boundaries, particularly for culturally "normal" individuals (whether they be Indian men or American women). Accordingly, the permeable ego boundaries of individuals who mature in the autocentric setting are here regarded as structures adapted to that setting. In this view, final boundary structures do not necessarily represent compromises among contending instincts of the inner world; they can also be adaptations to and extensions of the boundary conformation of the individual's outer world.

I am maintaining that American women, like Indian men, are coordinated, *through their diffuse ego functioning*, to their particular version of the autocentric environment. Thus we can better understand the positive correlation, in American women, between relatively unclear personal boundaries and relatively high personal morale; both the high morale and the low boundaries register the same achievement: successful adaptation to the autocentric milieu. To make this argument convincing, I must also demonstrate that the "average expectable" milieu of a representative American woman is, like the personal milieu of the preliterate Indian, essentially autocentric in character.

The autocentric quality of preliterate life is engendered by physical isolation. The typical villager does not have much contact with foreigners, and his familiars are literally alternative versions of himself. In them he finds his own history, his own preoccupations, and his own values and beliefs. To the extent that his world extends him in this fashion, it is autocentric.

The world of the urban American woman—if her role is primarily domestic—can in the same sense be self-extending and autocentric. Even in the midst of the city the domestic environment is to some degree separate from its surroundings. As a distinct but informal subculture it reflects in large part the wishes, tastes, and schedules of the homemaker who is central to its maintenance. Furthermore, her children are quite literally extensions of herself, just as she is a physical extension of the mother who trained her for domesticity and motherhood. Like her mother, the homemaker deals in her domestic sphere with a world of her own making—a world that extends her and that thereby meets the criteria for autocentricity.

Female ego styles and generational conflict

Similarly, when the domestic woman moves beyond the home and into the neighborhood, she still moves in an autocentric world. In other women she finds something of her own values, major concerns, and understandings of how best to handle those concerns. Generally speaking, common experience, shared by many women within the confines of the courtyard, block, and neighborhood, also creates bases for identification that override the awareness of physical distinction and boundary. The pathways through the neighborhood are familiar, and events at points along the pathway are, within limits, predictable.

Thus, to the extent that the neighborhood provides tradition, extended family relationships, and clear physical boundaries, it can convey to the established resident the autocentric experience of living at the center of converging kinship ties and affectional bonds. As in a Navajo sheep camp or a Mayan village, in the female domestic world diffuse ego boundaries may be a necessary precondition for mastery and contentment. Firm ego boundaries could lead to alienation—to a rupture of empathic bonds with one's family and with the pleasant self-confirming cycles of domestic and neighborhood life.

A Comparison of the Autocentric and Allocentric Ego States

Because the allocentric and the autocentric ego states will be continually referred to in the following discussion, I will now summarize some of the major differences between the two orientations. The comparisons will deal with coordinates of experience—space and time, constancy and change, self and other—that are particularly dependent on the level of ego-boundary development.

Autocentric: Space

The autocentric ego seeks out and creates relatively closed and private domains that are boundaried at their perimeters but diffuse and amorphous within. Pathways through the autocentric space are experienced as converging toward

Allocentric: Space

The allocentric ego seeks out and creates open areas that permit movement, exploration, and surprise. In allocentric space pathways are either nonexistent or are made relevant only through purposeful action toward self-defined goals.

the self. Autocentric space is a setting for human interactions that are emotionally pertinent to the self.

Allocentric space is the setting for the expansive actions of powerful agents—machines, troops of soldiers, flooding rivers—and for the actions of those who seek to oppose and control such agents.

Autocentric: Time

Autocentric time is linked to concrete events and cycles. A person judges where he is, timewise, according to the point he has reached in a familiar action sequence. Thus time is defined by a personal schedule in regard to some familiar activity. Attention is fixed on immediate events, not on intangible, still unreal, future events.

Allocentric: Time

Allocentric time is abstracted from the events that are ordered by it. It is a fixed standard, against which variable events are compared and measured. Time for the performance of present actions is regulated according to the time remaining for the completion of the total program.

Autocentric: Constancy and Change

The autocentric orientation is toward predictability. Thus one's wishes and expectations for future events are confirmed by the ordering and nature of the events themselves. The person's sense of self-continuity is tied to a redundant world that confirms his preconceptions about the way things are and ought to be in his chosen and familiar domain. A stable world means a stable self.

Allocentric: Constancy and Change

The allocentric orientation is toward seeking unexpected and surprising events that require an effective response. Such tests lead to a self-conception founded on the awareness of trustworthy inner resources. Predictability resides in the self and not in the environment. A stable self is abstracted from a changing world.

Autocentric: Self and Other

In the tightly knit and emotionally charged autocentric

Allocentric: Self and Other

A persistent sense of self-other distinctions is likely to be

Female ego styles and generational conflict

85

domain, enduring relationships among friends, kin, and enemies arouse, focus, and maintain important motives and their attendant affects. The person feels strongly about others and often interprets their behaviors and affects as being reactive to and reciprocal to his own longing, fear, or rage. He *predicts* the other in terms of the wishes, fears, and fantasies he bears toward him. He sees the complement, the denial, or the elaboration of his own emotion in the object of that emotion. Accordingly, when persistent interaction takes place around shared emotions, there is necessarily a blurring of self-other distinctions and of ego boundaries. The external world becomes, to some degree, an implicit metaphor of his feelings toward it. The object changes according to the emotional context in which it is experienced.

generated and maintained by unpredictable settings—by a "world one never made." In this relatively alienated setting, the person is constantly reminded of self-other discontinuities: of purpose, fantasy, and interpretation. He learns that he can achieve personal goals only by dealing with agents that have direction, logic, and structure of their own. He knows that he cannot, merely by wish or fantasy, influence the world beyond the immediate boundaries of his self. He experiences the object or agent "out there" as having a relatively constant nature, despite his shifting feelings toward it. The self is also objectified, reviewed from the perspectives of the "other," and revised accordingly.

Autocentric: Instrumentality

The world is dealt with "ritually." The person pantomimes in his own behavior the state he wishes to bring about in the world at large: Loving thoughts will lead to a peaceful world; weakness in a victim will induce mercy in an oppressor. Outgoing action is more expressive of inner rather than situational demands.

Allocentric: Instrumentality

The person assumes—especially in unfamiliar situations—that the other acts on the basis of alien, unpredictable principles. He resorts to "scientific" exploration to elucidate what these may be. Instrumentality is also turned against the self in the form of self-control and self-discipline. The self is revised in adaptation to new circumstances.

Autocentric: Morality

The autocentric person is responsive to the *immediate* needs, frustrations, and hurts of those he feels close to. He values no principle that, in its implementation, causes pain to himself or to those he identifies with: Wars are fought to hurt and kill a mother's child. Actions taken to relieve personal pain, or the pain of affiliates, create their own legitimacy: A law can be flouted because of its evident inhumanity.

Allocentric: Morality

The allocentric person is oriented toward the creation and service of *principles*. These principles are abstracted from concrete situations, referred to for guidance in concrete situations, and valued at least in part *because* they are abstract and assert man's ordering mind in the face of shifting events. Any law must be obeyed—*because it is a law*—until it is removed by lawful process.

Alienation and Autocentricity

I have asserted that the autocentric ego state, although usually associated with femininity, is not exclusive to that sex. Moreover, the empirical association between physical "femaleness" and autocentricity may reflect nurture more than nature. The value—if not the truth—of this contention is that it helps me understand certain aspects of modern alienation, particularly as it is manifested among young men who have been trained for productive roles in our society.

The autocentric orientation is appearing to a striking degree among men in Western society and seems to be both the cause and the correlate of masculine alienation. For whatever reasons, it is clear that the individuating, allocentric style is now regarded as the competitor rather than the complement of the autocentric style, and it is being discarded by some men in favor of autocentricity. The intrinsic, biological bases of masculinity have presumably remained constant—there is no reason to believe otherwise—and yet an ego style that was relegated mainly to women is becoming increasingly widespread among discontented young men of the affluent, postindustrial West. For example, I now find the same diffuse ego style that I had first located among women, and later among Indians, in the population of the Hippie world that fringes the Ann Arbor

Female ego styles and generational conflict

campus. I have been interviewing these alienated young men concerning their use of drugs, the meaning of the drug experience for them, and other pertinent life issues.

I am not now concerned with alienated, New Left *activists*, who are highly sensitive to pragmatic boundaries, particularly those between themselves and decisive power. The activists are not against boundaries per se but want to have the valued external power located within their own boundaries. They legitimize their demands through identification with others who have, in suffering, staked out their own moral claim to power: the blacks, the North Vietnamese, and so on. Rather, I am referring to the passive "Flower Children," who are more concerned with existential limitations—of mortality, history, selfhood, sex—than with inequalities in the distribution of social power. This group does not attempt to deal with boundaries and limitations through the use of force but through indirect and obsessively self-centered means. They change their *perception* of the boundary and revise it *projectively*, rather than instrumentally. That is, they revoke social and existential boundaries and limitations by ignoring them or by setting up hidden niches in which the usual boundaries do not obtain.

Thus for the Hippie culture the enemy is not really the power structure of society; it is "the great necessities of life." Although these youths may politicize their struggle against existential limitations by claiming that death is an invention of the Establishment, their essential argument is with the fate that has assigned them a single life, a single body, a single sex, a single set of parents, and an irreversible history. To have a self—boundaried and distinguished from other selves—is limitation; to be male—to have a sex that was genetically determined without any personal choice—is an insult and a restriction; to have a history—to realize that one is already limited and determined by his own prior choices or by choices made for him—is to experience unacceptable boundaries and limitations regarding future options. History is to be abolished because it reminds us of our beginning, of our time-boundedness, and of our end—our mortal fate.

Feminine Personality & Conflict

If the opposition to existential boundaries is a feminine ego trait, then the antiboundary weaponry of the alienated is also feminine. Dress and personal cosmetics are important boundary abolishers: Through long hair, beads, and flowers these youths claim title to a femininity that was boundaried off from them, as they see it, without prior consultation. Symbolically, dress also wipes out history: Although they were born middle-class WASPs or Jews, they can *dress* as though they were blacks, Hell's Angels, cowboys, Indians, women, or all of these types at once. Also through their dress, the alienated claim title to all the good, striking, and powerful elements in the world.[5] Accordingly, dress revokes the ultimate boundary of the self—at least that version of the self that implies a coherent agent organized around central themes and goals. Such self-consistency is a threat to the Hippie because it forecloses too many possibilities. In reaction, he uses his collage of garments and cosmetics to symbolically incorporate all those options—masculine and feminine, psychopathic and sensitive—that have generally been regarded by the square world as mutually exclusive. Thus the Hippies use clothing as women do: to attract attention, to renew themselves, to try on alternative and even conflicting selves, and, most importantly, to do away with the intolerable boundary between fantasy and actuality. They feel they are whatever they choose to wear.

Indeed, all major features of the Hippie scene mime the wish to lose boundaries and to restore the autocentric world. Certainly driving rock music and flickering light shows, which the alienated now favor, override the boundaries between the sound, the light, and the actions that they propel; that is, the stimulus and the response are fused in a continuous experience. More importantly, group experiences—whether they involve groping or talking—break down individual-communal boundaries so that each participant's body and psychic contents become part of the collective property. The group, like the wardrobe, becomes a repository of experiences and of selves that are available to any member willing to pool his body and his inner life in the communal hive. These collectivist perspectives are now being institutionalized in various communes, which involve a total offensive against individuation and especially against the alienating interpersonal boundaries that individuation necessarily involves. A kind of psychic com-

---

[5] This total ecumenism is well illustrated by the response of the prominent Hippie poet and guru Allen Ginsberg to Kramer's (1968, p. 38) question concerning his religion: "Ginsberg said that he was probably a Buddhist Jew with attachments to Krishna, Siva, Allah, Coyote, and the Sacred Heart. Then he said no—he was simply on a sort of pilgrimage, 'shopping around.' " Religion becomes a matter of supermarket consumption, rather than commitment.

munism prevails in these settlements that goes far beyond the pooling of goods and labor—to the sharing of mates, children, paternity, and psychic "energies." [6]

Drugs are especially valued because they provide a direct experience of boundary loss and diffusion for the alienated. My subjects report concrete experiences of sinking into the floor, of merging with the walls, and of becoming the cup that they hold while being able to look back and see themselves holding it. Drugs make the world autocentric in the most fundamental sense, and it is in regard to drugs that we most directly encounter the mythic view of the self that propels the autocentric revolutions of our time. The self is depicted as divided between a corrupted ego—the outpost of the Establishment within one's head—and a pure inner life—a reservoir of coherence, natural wisdom, and life-bestowing energies. Accordingly, for those who hold to this myth, automatic legitimacy is granted to any agent or practice (drugs, mod clothing, communes, encounter groups) that presumably does away with limiting inter- or intrapersonal boundaries and thereby allows the individual to recapture the treasury of authentic selves and sensibilities that he has been exiled from by his ego. Once this "Rousseauism of the inner life" is adopted, the revolutionary rhetoric is turned inward. The Establishment ego is to be rooted out, like a kind of psychic cancer, so that renewal can take place; and drugs, the Molotov cocktail of this internal liberation, automatically acquire legitimacy and even holiness. I would argue that the myths of the autocentric revolution are *feminine* metaphors. The undeniable capacity of women to grow babies in the womb has as a mythic counterpart the idea of an inner life that is intrinsically perfect, naturally wise, and life enhancing. Like a woman, the alienated drug user looks inside himself for new life and for rebirth.

Autocentric Mothers and Alienated Sons

The similarity in the boundary functions of American women and Indian men reflects their membership in psychoso-

---

[6] The Hippies have discovered the equivalence between their own autocentricity and that of preliterate Indians. Their communes are often called *tribes*, and in them Indian social organization, rituals, food, and dress are extensively copied. The Hippies have made culture heroes out of American Indians precisely because they represent the autocentric virtues of community, unity with nature, and lack of individual striving.

cial environments that pattern self-other experience in equivalent, autocentric ways. But why should alienated American males be attracted to and reproduce the autocentric domain and life style? They certainly did not grow up within the redundant world of tribe and isolated village; and presumably their "official" masculine socialization, at home and in school, has had the aim of preparing them for participation in boundaried, distinct, and linear domains. The usual models of socialization and of individual-social relationships would not have led us to predict this swing toward autocentricity and do not provide an understanding of it now.

In the absence of a comprehensive theory of personal-social relationships, a body of data and observation is being generated that may help to account for some of the contrasts between the middle-class alienated youth and his more conventional class and age peer. I refer mainly to Keniston's (1965) study of alienated youth and secondarily to my own interviews with male drug users. These pieces of evidence suggest that alienated American males have indeed received an unofficial but intense autocentric socialization that is at odds with their formal sex-role training. Depth investigation of such individuals frequently reveals an unrelinquished, "umbilical" tie with a mother who is perceived by the son as intense, seductive, and unsatisfied. The father is at least psychologically absent, for both the son and the mother. In compensation, the mother typically intensifies her tie with the son. The normal boundaries of the mother-son relationship are abridged, resulting in a kind of matching between the unconscious, erotic fantasies of both the mother and the son. This matching is detrimental to the son's capacity to form stable ego boundaries between himself and any agent that is emotionally important to him.

Under more normal circumstances the son comes to apprehend that his mother's love is not only for him, that she has an existence apart from him, and that he too continues to exist when her attention and affection are turned toward others. In this manner he learns that his wishes and fantasies do not predict to their relevant objects—there is an object world separate from himself. Fantasy becomes an inner dimension—recognized as such—not a representation that mingles the undifferentiated inner and outer realms.

For the potentially alienated child the self-other distinction is blurred over. The mother's autocentric styles foster perceptual and cognitive styles in the son, with the result that he too favors intuition over investigation, appreciation ("digging it") over understanding, and emotional demonstrations over instrumental action.

The symbiotic mother-son bond also transmits her own specific personal myths and self-representations. The self-conception of the alienated youth is a translation of his mother's fantasy about herself. Her personal myth is that she has sold out her creative gift in exchange for the tainted security offered by a man unworthy of her sacrifice. Given the fuzziness of autocentric boundaries, it is easy for the mother to assign to her husband the responsibility for her own "corruption." By a similar magic she can cast the son into her psychodrama as a representation of her still uncompromised and wondrous younger self. If the symbiotic ties, as well as the son's natural Oedipal loyalties, are strong enough, he too will come to see himself in terms of his mother's myth: He too is a person of infinite promise who is being forced to sell out to a corrupt Establishment—his father's world—that offers nothing in exchange but a deathlike, shameful security.

The symbiotic maternal union can be a viable arrangement for the son if it intersects with appropriate sex roles. Often, however, it does not. When the boy goes to college, he is fully exposed—often for the first time—to a world that has been crafted largely by and for men. It is a world of rules, of impersonal standards impersonally enforced, of isolated individual endeavor, and of rationality rather than emotion. In this allocentric world the alienated boy, with his long history of autocentric maternal union and identification, is truly a misfit. His usual response is to drop out—that is, to retreat to a world of basement apartments, of intimate relationships resonant with "vibrations," and of communication intensified by drugs. In effect, he reconstructs an autocentric world that does not require the usual allocentric instrumentalities and that therefore does not sponsor the usual allocentric distinctions between fantasy and reality. By doing nothing in his dropout world, he preserves the illusion that he *could* do or be everything. Unlike his mother, who traded too much for too little, he will not commit himself finally to any relationship, role, or identity that is not completely "worthy" of him.

Thus the alienated make social ecologies and social causes out of both the form and the content of the maternal ego. That is, they reproduce the unbounded world that she represented to them. Their slogans register their mothers' complaints against the hyperrational, dehumanized world of their fathers: "Do not fold, spindle, or mutilate me." "Make love, not war." "Stop killing babies." Likewise, in the alienated students' condemnations of the universities as degree factories where students are taught to foreclose their infinite potential in exchange for security, we gather that they have politicized their mothers' charges against the infuriatingly rational and achievement-centered fathers.

Certainly the mother's grievances do not completely determine the politics of her alienated son. His complaints are also supported by his peers and initiated by older *male* ideologists, whose critiques of society are often valid. Yet it does appear that a mother's complaints against her personal lot, and particularly against her husband, will emerge in the next generation's politics of alienation and rebellion.

Boundary Development: Intrinsic and Extrinsic Influences

Environmental influences that regulate individual experiences of self and other—the domestic-neighborhood milieu, the tribal-village milieu, the intense and seductive mother—all appear to be capable of generating autocentric ego functions. When males are extensively exposed to the boundary-diffusing tribal or maternal influences, they are as likely as women to deal with the world in autocentric terms.

Although the autocentric and allocentric ego states may be more directly tied to environment than to biological sex, there do appear to be fixed and intrinsic sex differences that have psychic representation and that steer men and women toward environments that subsequently shape the ego functions. Thus the research of Erikson (1963, pp. 97–108) and of Brenneis (1967) indicates that there are clear sex preferences in terms of action, object, and the environmental setting of action.

Erikson showed that boys and girls of the same age, supplied with the same toys and play space, constructed strikingly different environments. Girls typically interpreted the play space as the interior of a house, which was defined by a circle of furniture and within which people communed, worked, and amused themselves. This space was often invaded by something threatening—"a pig" or "Daddy riding a lion." Boys turned the same available space into an outside world defined

Female ego styles and generational conflict

by towers and streets, and they "channeled the traffic of cars, animals, and Indians" through the world. The human figure that boys most commonly used was the "policeman" doll—a symbol of regulation by impersonal laws.

Brenneis' research on sex differences in dreaming makes a similar point: The male-female differences that Erikson found in regard to the location and scope of the "play space" were replicated for the "dream space." Again, the masculine themes of conflict, threat, and expansive movement were typically enacted in outdoor dream settings; the feminine themes, usually involving personal encounters of various sorts, were more typically played out in enclosed dream settings.

As a psychoanalyst, Erikson stresses the psychosexual determinants of the contrasting play of boys and girls. He speculates that the boy's conception of space as the setting for expansive movements and for active, tall, and thrusting agents takes its form from the phallic-intrusive organization of male body parts, musculature, and attendant instincts. The girl's concern with the furnishing and protection of *internal* space reflects a body image centered on sensitive, receptive, and inwardly based procreative equipment.[7] However, while the two sexes gravitate to milieux that are congenial to their intrinsic psychosexual dispositions, these ecologies and the experiences that they provide will *incidentally* sponsor or retard the formation of ego boundaries. The two sexes choose their relevant objects and environments but not the developed ego-boundary structures that will be sponsored by those preferred environments.

The Autocentric Revolution

The potential independence of psychosexual preferences from developed ego styles may underlie the current redistribution of autocentricity and allocentricity. The young boy can make the distinctly masculine choice to love his mother and identify with her against his father, and as a consequence he

---

[7] In further support of the contention that "maleness" and "femaleness" have intrinsic spatial or ecological referents, Erikson (1964) has presented observations of subhuman primate groups. The males typically ranged the perimeters of their territory—and sometimes sought to extend them—whereas the females, particularly during emergencies, clustered toward the center of the territory or band.

may receive her feminine, low-boundary orientation. By the same token, a provocatively feminine daughter can co-opt her father's attention, share his most intimate thoughts, and inherit his allocentric, masculine ego style. Thus the tensions between parents in the contemporary family not only may give rise to a high divorce rate but may also contribute to the contemporary crossover of what used to be sex-specific ego styles. When parents seek allies among their children, the parental division can be replicated internally by their offspring as a split between masculine drives and the diffuse, autocentric ego or between feminine instincts and the isolating, allocentric ego. Inevitably, psychological clinics fill up with youths who refuse to renounce their claim on the prerogatives and styles of the other sex but who, at the same time, bemoan their lack of identity.

The autocentric revolution cannot stem from marital discord alone; since it is now worldwide, it must have a basis in wider social conditions as well. It appears that the allocentric ego has conquered nature and, in so doing, has reduced the condition of necessity, scarcity, and consequent patriarchy that was its chief support. The stern exercise of allocentric discipline may have brought us to a condition so secure that we can cease to monitor reality as vigilantly as before. Instead, we can relax into the autocentric situation of permitting our wishes about reality to determine its management and evaluation. Meanwhile, the inherent passivity of this withdrawal from the allocentric to the autocentric state of mind is masked by the rhetoric of revolution—that is, by claims that regression is actually progression and that the move toward autocentricity constitutes a "life-enhancing" rebellion against the allocentric "death culture."

Thus current revolutions are led by once discredited autocentric constituencies—priests, artists, blacks, women, bohemians—and are directed less against social injustice than against the allocentric state of mind. In large degree they derive their content and their slogans ("love," "soul," "flower power") from the autocentric ego, and they are aimed at undoing intrapersonal and interpersonal boundaries, mutually exclusive categories, and linear thought. The inherent contradiction of impersonal, mass society seems to be that it does not nurture the allocentric ego that it requires for its continuation. We do not yet know if the increasing gap between personal and social requirements will lead to a revision of our institutions along

Female ego styles and generational conflict

more human-centered lines. It is a hopeful possibility. However, the more *likely* possibility is that the autocentric revolution will pave the way for a dictatorship of the remaining managers, who will be eager to use the power conceded to them by default.

References

Brenneis, B. Differences in male and female ego style in manifest dream content. Unpublished doctoral dissertation, University of Michigan, 1967.

Erikson, E. *Childhood and society* (2nd ed.) New York: Norton, 1963.

Erikson, E. Reflections on womanhood. *Daedalus,* Spring 1964.

Freud, S. Some psychological consequences of the anatomical differences between the sexes (1925). *Collected papers,* Vol. 5: *Miscellaneous papers, 1888–1938.* London: Hogarth Press, 1950. Pp. 186–197.

Gutmann, D. An exploration of ego configurations in middle and later life. In B. Neugarten (Ed.), *Personality in middle and later life.* New York: Atherton, 1964. Pp. 114–148.

Gutmann, D. "On cross-cultural studies as a naturalistic approach in psychology." *Human Development*, 1967, **10,** 187–198.

Keniston, K. *The uncommitted.* New York: Harcourt, 1965.

Kramer, J. Paterfamilias. *The New Yorker,* Aug. 16, 1968. Pp. 32–73.

Schachtel, E. *Metamorphosis.* New York: Basic Books, 1959.

index

Abortion, spontaneous, 18
Achievement
   and aggression, 56–57
   vs. femininity, 45–46, 54–57, 61, 67–72
   negative consequences for women, 54–57, 67–68
   success avoidance, in same sex vs. coed schools, 71–72
   (*See also* Achievement anxiety; Achievement motivation.)
Achievement anxiety, 54–58
   concern about femininity, 61
   denial of achievement, 61–62
   fear of social rejection, 60
   fear-of-success imagery, 46–47, 64–67
   studies of, 59–67
   (*See also* Achievement motivation.)
Achievement motivation, 46–72
   arousal, 51–52
   assessment, 51
   vs. attitudes of significant men, 69–70

Achievement motivation (continued)
   Expectancy-Value theory, 47
   marriage vs. career conflict, 67–68
   n Achievement, 46
   and peer pressure, 69–70
   and performance, 53
   sex differences, 48–53
   and social acceptability, 52
   Theory of Achievement Motivation, 47–48, 53
   (*See also* Achievement; Achievement anxiety.)
Adelson, J., 36, 38
Adolescence
   cultural pressures during, 38–42
   development of sex identity, 8–9
   like-sexed friendships, 35–36, 37
   psychological aspects, boys vs. girls, 31–42
   search for self-identity, 32–33
   sexual fantasy during, 36–37
   sexual inhibition, 8–9

Affect change and menstrual cycle, 21–26
Alienated sons, and autocentric mothers, 90–93
Alienated youth
  autocentricity of, 77, 87–90
  drug use, 90
  opposition to existential boundaries, 88–90
Allocentric ego style, 77–96
Allocentric society, ego boundaries in, 82
Amenorrhea, 18, 34
Angelini, A. L., 52
Anxiety
  in interpersonal relationships, 37–38
  about physiological developments, 7–8, 36–37
  and use of the Pill, 15–17, 25–26
Aristotle, 54
Asayama, S., 36
Atkinson, J. W., 47, 48, 49, 50, 51, 53
Autocentric ego style, 77–96
Autocentric mothers and alienated sons, 90–93
Autocentric revolution, 94–96
Autocentric society, ego boundaries in, 80–82
Autocentricity of alienated youth, 77, 87–90

Balzac, Honoré de, 62
Bardwick, J. M., 14, 20–21, 23–25, 33, 34, 37
Barker, R. G., 31
Behrman, S. J., 20–21
Benedek, T., 7–8, 22–23
Boutourline-Young, H., 31

Boys
  development of independence, 4
  development of sexuality, 5–6
Brenneis, B., 93, 94

Career vs. marriage conflict, 67–68
Cervix, premature dilation of, 18
Clark, R. A., 48, 51
Coleman, J. G., 39–40
Coppen, A., 22

Dalton, K., 22
Dating, 9, 37–38
Death Anxiety scores, premenstrual vs. at ovulation, 23, 24
Denial defense mechanisms
  and reproductive system changes, 17–18
  and use of the Pill, 15–16
Denial of achievement, 61–62
Dependency relationships in girls, 4–5
Deutsch, H., 43
Diffuse Anxiety scores, premenstrual vs. at ovulation, 23
Douvan, E., 33, 35, 36, 38
Drug use by alienated youth, 90
Dysmenorrhea, 18, 34

Ego boundaries
  in the allocentric society, 82
  in the autocentric society, 80–82

Ego boundaries (continued)
　cultural and societal effects on, 80–82, 93
　diffuse, of women, 82–84
　and group experiences, 89–90
　sex differences in development of, 93–94
　of women in the domestic role, 82–84
Ego psychology
　among American Indians, 80–82
　men vs. women, 78–80
Ego styles
　autocentric and allocentric, 77–96
　comparison, 84–87
　"boundaried" and "unboundaried" women, 79
Ehrmann, W., 14
Erikson, E., 32, 93, 94,
Expectancy-Value theory of motivation, 47

False pregnancy, 18–19
Feather, N. T., 47, 50, 53
Fels Research Institute studies on sex role, 39
Femininity vs. individual achievement, 45–46, 54–57, 67–72
Field, W. F., 52
Field dependence, of boys vs. girls, 34
French, E. G., 48, 53
Freud, S., 53, 56, 78
Friedenberg, E. Z., 40–41
Friendships, like-sexed, in adolescence, 35–36, 37

Gebhard, P. H., 10, 36
Ginsberg, Allen, 89
Gleser, G. C., 23
Gold, M., 33
Gottschalk, L. A., 23
Gottschalk's Verbal Anxiety Scale, in study of mood changes during menstrual cycle, 23–26
Group experiences and ego boundaries, 89–90
Guilt Anxiety scores, premenstrual vs. at ovulation, 23
Gutmann, D., 41, 79, 80

Harvard Crimson, 71
Hippies
　autocentricity of, 87–90
　protest against sex-role prescriptions, 41
　similarity to Indians, 90
Horner, M., 59, 65
Horrocks, J. E., 37
Hostility level and use of the Pill, 25–26
Housman, H., 22

Independence, development of, in boys vs. girls, 4–5
Indian societies, autocentricity of, 80–82
Ivey, M. E., 23–25, 33, 37

Javert, C., 18
Johnson, V. E., 11, 13

Kagan, J., 39, 57
Kaye, C., 33
Kelly, J. V., 18
Keniston, K., 91

Kessel, N., 22
Kinsey, A. C., 10, 36
Komarowsky, M., 69
Kramer, J., 89
Krawitz, R., 52

Labor, premature, 18
Lactation, negative feelings about, 7
Lesser, G. S., 52, 53
Like-sexed friendships in adolescence, 35–36, 37
Lipinski, B. G., 53
Litwin, G. H., 48, 53
Lowell, E. L., 48, 51
Luce, Clare Booth, 54

Maccoby, E. E., 55
Mahone, C., 48
Mannes, M., 55
Marriage vs. career conflict, 67–68
Martin, C. E., 10, 36
Masters, W. H., 11, 13
Masturbation, 9
McClelland, D. C., 45, 48, 49–50, 51–52
Mead, M., 32, 45, 55, 56
Menarche, 32 (*See also* Menstrual cycle; Menstruation.)
Menstrual cycle
  high-estrogen vs. low-estrogen and testosterone phases, 22–23
  mood changes during, 21–26, 33–34
  psychological studies of women using the Pill, 25–26
  (*See also* Menstruation.)

Menstrual taboos, 7–8
Menstruation
  dysfunctions, 17–18, 34
  negative feelings about, 7–8
  physiological changes during, 32
  psychological aspects of, 32–35
  (*See also* Menstrual cycle.)
Mood changes and menstrual cycle, 21–26, 33–34
Moos, R. H., 22
Moss, H. A., 39, 57
Mothers, autocentric, and alienated sons, 90–93
Motivation, achievement, 46–72
Murray, H. A., et al., 36
Mussen, P. H., 31
Mutilation anxiety
  premenstrual, 24–25
  premenstrual vs. at ovulation, 23
My Fair Lady, 54

n Achievement, 46
Newcomb, T., 40

Oral contraceptives, psychological consequences of use, 14–17, 25–26
Orgasm achievement, in women, 9–13
Ovulation (*See* Menstrual cycle.)

Pacing, developmental, boys vs. girls, 31
Packard, R., 52

Index

100

COLLEGE FOR HUMAN SERVICES
LIBRARY
345 HUDSON STREET
NEW YORK, N.Y. 10014

Paige, K. E., 25–26
Passive dependent women, reproductive system changes in, 17–21
Peer group values, sex-role differences, 39–40
Peer pressure and achievement goals, 69–70
Personality changes during menstrual cycle, 21–26, 33–34
Pill, the, studies of women using, 14–17, 25–26
Pomeroy, W. B., 10, 36
Pregnancy
  false pregnancy (pseudocyesis), 18–19
  negative feelings about, 7
  psychosomatic disorders of, 18
Premarital sex, 13–17
Premenstrual mood changes, 21–26, 33–34
Prepuberty, development of sex identity during, 5–7
Prostitution anxieties, 15–17
Pseudocyesis, 18–19
Psychosomatic changes in reproductive system, 17–21

Reproductive system
  ambivalence toward, 3–17
  psychosomatic disorders of, 17–21
  studies of uterine contractions, 20–21
Riesman, D., 56, 68
Rossi, A., 57
Rubenstein, B., 22–23

Sanford, N., 55, 67
Sanford, R. N., 36, 40
Schachtel, E., 77
Schaefer, L., 12
Schwenn, M., 69
Scott, W. A., 59
Self-esteem, 3–5
  changes during menstrual cycle, 21–23
Self-identity, search for, in adolescence, 32–33
Separation Anxiety scores, premenstrual vs. at ovulation, 23
Sex identity, development of, 5–6, 8–9
Sex roles, cultural norms and pressures, 38–42
Sexual development
  pacing, 31
  psychological conflicts in, 31–42
Sexuality
  in adolescence, 8–9
  arousal, 10–13
  orgasmic response, in female, 9–13
  premarital, 13–17
  sexual fantasy during adolescence, 36–37
Shainess, N., 7, 22
Shame Anxiety scores, premenstrual vs. at ovulation, 23
Sherfy, M. J., 13
Springer, K. J., 23
Stewart, I., 21–22
Stone, C. P., 31
Sutherland, H., 21–22
Symonds, P. M., 36

Tangri, S., 33, 69
Thompson, G. G., 37

Unmarried women, conflicts
 in sex life of, 13–17
Uterine contractions,
 studies of, 20–21

Vaginismus, 18
Veroff, J., 51

Wallin, P., 10
Whittier, John Greenleaf, 72
Wilcox, S., 51
Williams, J., 33
Winterbottom, M. R., 45
Witkin, H. A., 34

Zweben, J. E., 14